Jerrod's words pierce the generational gaps providing fresh perspectives and applicable truths. He may not have lived through all of the different generations (yet), but he speaks confidently and accurately through them all. This is a must read for everyone. We all face challenges as we collaborate with people of all ages. Jerrod not only helps us see the differences, but he also provides practical steps to forge better communication and deeper relationships.

– KIN THOMPSON

University Professor
Proud Baby Boomer

From feeling seen and heard to being intriguingly challenged in thought and leadership, Jerrod's perspective and voice towards Gen Z may be one that creates an oasis of middle ground between all generations, allowing us to see eye-to-eye for the first time in, you know, maybe ever. While Jerrod highlights the intricate patterns of generational gaps from a Gen X worldview, I truly believe this is a must read for those in the shoes of a Gen Zer who feels the older generations don't quite understand. Maybe they do and we've simply needed a reality check to see where they're coming from. From 8-Track to Emoji is that necessary reality check, and may be one of the only ways to move forward in effective cross-generation collaboration. Especially in the workspace.

– ADAM RAGSDALE, GEN Z

CEO of The VOCA app

Maybe kids being kids isn't such a bad thing

FROM

8-TRACK

TO

EMOJI

THE SECRET TO CROSS-GENERATIONAL LEADERSHIP

JERROD MURR

Prepared for publication by www.40DayPublishing.com

Cover design by www.40DayGraphics.com

Printed in the United States of America

CONTENTS

PART 1

GENERATIONS, TENDENCIES, AND BIAS

CHAPTER 1: A HOUSE DIVIDED

What You, Me, and Socrates Have in Common.

"Children; they have bad manners, contempt for authority; they show disrespect for elders and love chatter in the place of exercise. They no longer rise when elders enter the room, they contradict their parents and tyrannize their teachers. Children are now tyrants."

Keep reading to find out who said this. You may be surprised.

A HOUSE DIVIDED

Welcome to the great divide.

Well, not *the* great divide, but a great divide anyway.

Perhaps not a great divide, but a divide, nonetheless.

This divide isn't new. It just feels like it. Trust me, we all feel it.

Baby Boomers, Generation X, Millennials, Generation Z.

We all feel the divide. We feel the generational gap.

You may or may not feel the gap to the extent of your neighbor.

I suppose that is why I described it as the great divide, then hesitated.

It is a great divide for many.

A small divide for some.

A divide for all of us.

It seems the gap is widening. The noticeable differences between generations are more flagrant.

Maybe it's because of the speed of technology.

Maybe it's the amount of information we process.

Maybe it's the memes.

Whatever causes it, it exists.

It specifically exists in the workforce as it becomes increasingly difficult to lead team members from various generations.

The Boomers are out of touch,

the Xers are angry and disenchanted,

the Millennials are entitled,

and the kids are just kids.

(My apologies to all of you Gen Z reading this. Don't worry, just keep reading. I think you are

fantastic, mostly, and I will brag on you throughout the book.)

In fact, I hope many Gen Z are reading this. This book isn't just for old people. This book is about cross-generational leadership. Younger leaders leading those older than themselves. Older leaders leading those younger than themselves.

Some of us feel young and misjudged because of our age.

Some of us feel old and misjudged because of our age.

Age is relative. This book is designed for leaders of all ages.

We will look at all of these generational stereotypes and learn some generalizations we may not know.

We will look at all equally from Gen Z to Boomers.

We won't begrudge or bemoan any specific generation too much. Unless you are listening to this for free, ripped off some site and shared with you by your friend…

I'm just kidding. *(But, really, you couldn't even buy the book?)*

In all seriousness, the generational divide is great. We have a meme for every boomer, a stereotype for every age, and a criticism for every generation.

We are either too quick or too slow to adopt technology.

Some don't like the office, while others can only work from the office.

Many hate office hours, while others believe real accountability exists only in proximity.

The generational gap causes problems for the workplace.

We have cross-generational issues.

But these differences are not new.

The gap has always existed.

That's where the quote — remember the one from earlier? — comes in.

"Children; they have bad manners, contempt for authority; they show disrespect for elders and love chatter in the place of exercise. They no longer rise when elders enter the room, they contradict their parents and tyrannize their teachers. Children are now tyrants."

- Socrates

Socrates?!?

Yes, Socrates. *That* Socrates.

This is not some new quote from a fundamental extremist who thinks the world is at its end. This is not a quote from a mid-twentieth-century psychologist promoting a new way to properly raise children.

This is not some prose from a Victorian-era elitist who believes children should be seen and not heard.

This is not a colonial purist who does not spare the rod to spoil the child.

This is an ancient Greek philosopher from about 400 BC claiming *then* that children are *now* tyrants.

As you walk backward through the timeline of humanity, we can imagine people from every era agreeing with Socrates.

The quote illustrates the eternal existence of a generational gap.

This book is about that generation gap.

This book is about ageism.

This book is about those awful old people.

This book is about those terrible young people.

The young will always view the old with some contempt.

The old will always view the young with some disdain.

"Youth will always be wasted on the young."

"Parents just don't understand."

Thank you, George Bernard Shaw and Fresh Prince, respectively.

Therefore, we do not have just a generational issue.

We have a leadership issue.

We always have.

WHY THIS MATTERS

Every generation, at any given point, is given a stereotype.

Crazy enough, stereotypes are often transferred to the next generation.

For example, it's not simply that young people in the twenty-first century are disrespectful and lazy.

Young people in the 1990s were lazy.

Young people in the 1960s were disrespectful.

When defining generations with certain characteristics we are, in fact, merely describing young people.

We have been describing young people in the same way for centuries *(Remember the Socrates quote?)*.

The flip side, of course, is the disregard in which young people hold older generations.

Boomers are entrenched in their way of doing things.

Boomers are reluctant to change.

Boomers don't embrace younger people in leadership roles.

Boomers are slow to adopt technology.

The irony, of course, is that the generations before Boomers were similarly described in the mid- and late-twentieth century…and way before that.

We aren't describing Baby Boomers as much as we are describing, well…old people…

Sorry, Boomers, *perceived* old people.

Old is always 20 years from now.

It is important to grasp the idea of the "Everlasting Generation Gap."

When we realize that generations across millennia have never really seen eye-to-eye, it gives us hope.

It means that, as a leader, I can do something.

Something different.

Something *better*.

It means that every generation isn't stuck with some never-before-seen set of characteristics that we just have to deal with.

It means that Baby Boomers are not inherently judgmental.

It means that Gen X is not inherently cynical.

It means Millennials are not inherently coddled.

It means that Gen Z may actually be able to communicate away from their phones.

When we see the generational gap as everlasting, we can move beyond the assumptions and stereotypes and start to lead people.

I can learn more about myself and others in order to be a cross-generational leader.

Are there some unique factors contributing to the general outlook of every generation? Yes.

But we are not bound by those as leaders.

In this book, we will look at emerging trends of upcoming generations.

We will consider common biases of established generations.

We will study the differences in generations to have a better appreciation and understanding.

We can then leave those stereotypes at the door and lead people well.

There is a generation gap.

There always will be.

But it behooves us all to stop bemoaning what has always existed and become better leaders instead.

SO, WHAT'S DIFFERENT NOW?

The short answer: speed and distance.

This book is an attempt to look at generational gaps and cross-generational leadership with fresh eyes. We are considering new ideas and a radical approach that may be simpler than we think and more personal than we ever believed.

No previous generation has considered an upcoming generation an improvement.

We typically don't like to believe that the next generation is better than us.

Most likely, you won't hear your parents or grandparents say your generation is smarter, kinder, wiser, or better prepared to lead than they were.

Instead, we often look at upcoming generations with righteous disdain.

We have a "holier than thou" outlook that doesn't remember the errors of our youth.

We forget that our parents and grandparents felt the same way about us.

That practice has not changed for thousands of years.

What *is* different is the speed of technology.

- Globally, there are about 1.35 million tech startups around the world.
- The number of smart devices collecting, analyzing, and sharing data should hit 50 billion by 2030.
- The global internet penetration rate in 2022 is around 63%.
- The computing and processing capacity of computers hits double figures every 18 months.
- The world will produce 463 exabytes of data by 2025.

- By 2030, 500 billion devices will be connected to the internet.[1]

Our technological advancement within the last thirty years is more than the last 10,000 years combined. Technological advancement is one of the reasons it becomes difficult to project the future development of younger generations. The unknown truly is unknown because the technology we know and use today will likely be obsolete in just a few short years. How will the integration of technology inform the ethos and mold the morays of younger people? Time will tell.

Today, emerging generations have less in common with older generations (than years past) because of technology. Even within emerging generations there is a divide due to individualized experiences with technological advancement.

The speed of technology may change the way we think about generations.

Here's what I mean:

A Millennial is anyone born from 1980 to 1996.[2] I am a Millennial, born in 1981. I did not get a cell phone until I graduated high school. I was a fully functioning adult, paying my own bills, when I chose to purchase an antiquated flip phone that could not even text.

---

[1] https://techjury.net/blog/how-fast-is-technology-growing/#gref
[2] Depends on who you ask. It's 1980*ish* to 1996*ish*.

12

One of our former Paradigm Shift[3] teammates, Zach, was born in the late 1980s. He too is a Millennial. He got a cell phone when he started driving. His parents bought it for him. His phone was a Nokia "brick" phone. (Still the best phone ever, by the way.) He could text and call, but it wasn't yet a "smart" phone. Finally, another co-worker, Kyle, was born in the last part of the Millennial generation in 1996. He got a smart cell phone in eighth grade. He spent the entirety of his teen years with access to the internet 24/7. All three of us have incredibly similar upbringings in the same area of the country, yet the speed of technology changes the way we perceive and interact in and with the world.

The other notable difference between previous emerging generations and today's emerging generations is connectedness.

As of 2022, there are 5 billion internet users.[4]

Social media is a daily part of our lives.

We can connect with a stranger across the globe as easily as we connect with our next-door neighbor.

Maybe even easier.

Is this good or bad?

---

[3] Paradigm Shift offers leadership training all over the world. You should hire us.
[4] https://techjury.net/blog/how-fast-is-technology-growing/#gref

Maybe both.

While in the grand scheme of humanity, social media's long-term effects cannot yet be gauged. We can all agree it has an effect. We can definitively say that upcoming generations are more connected now compared to any previous generation before them.

This connectedness shapes the way we perceive the world and interact with it.

That is what's different.

There has always been a generational gap.

But the speed of technology and our world's connectedness affects that gap differently than any other period of history.

What does this mean for cross-generational leaders?

It means there is a wider, faster-growing gap than in previous generations.

It means we need adaptability, vulnerability, and empathy.

We need new approaches.

We need new paradigms.

We need better leaders.

CHAPTER 2: GENERATION IDENTIFICATION

Happy Days, *Who's the Boss?*, or *Modern Family*

WHAT AM I???

What exactly is a Boomer?

What is a Millennial?

What is a generation?

These cannot be words thrown around with little regard.

As cross-generational leaders we must seek first to understand.

That begins with understanding current generational labels, potential tendencies, and where stereotypes may have started.

A generation is considered to be all of the people born and living at about the same time, collectively speaking. It can also be described as the average period, generally about thirty years, during which children are born and grow up, become adults, and begin to have children of their own.

In the workforce today, there are four generations actively working.

Baby Boomers I	1946-1954
Baby Boomers II	1955-1964
Generation X	1965-1980
Millennials	1981-1996
Generation Z	1997-2012

WHY DOES IT MATTER?

It matters because people matter. Names matter. Labels matter.

We lead people. We connect with people.

If we want to become better leaders, communicators, or capable business partners, we must work to understand people.

Anything that is used to divide people can be used to unite people.

Instead of seeing generational differences as inconvenient obstacles to be avoided, good leaders see generational differences as opportunities to learn, connect and discover identity.

But that isn't our default setting.

Our default setting is often dismissive, critical, or judgmental.

Each generation looks at others and makes sweeping generalizations.

These generalizations become stereotypes.

Stereotypes become frames of reference that are oversimplified images of people.

While there may be some generalized truths among individuals in a specific generation, we cannot apply them to all people within that generation.

Culture, environment, and other factors, like birth order, social and economic status, and living conditions, form a person's outlook, persona, work ethic, and more. To say all Boomers are afraid of technology is no more accurate than saying all Millennials hate to work.

In this book, we examine the stereotypical associations of both established and emerging generations and flesh out the individual truths that are more accurate. If we stick only to the stereotypes, we run the risk of miscommunication and more significant gaps than we perceive now…or worse. Much worse.

GENERATION IDENTIFICATION

Generations are typically identified by numbers or dates. Maybe when you were born, when you started having kids, or what age you are today.

Perhaps even more relevant than the dates we are born, however, are the generational markers we most identify with as individuals.

There are three major factors that influence our generational identification and thus our worldview: major social events, pop culture, and technology.

MAJOR SOCIAL EVENTS

Think about what defined your childhood from around age five to eleven. What major world event happened that stands out in your memory?

For most, it is probably the first event you remember that caused you to stop and pay attention.

Do you remember exactly where you were when John F. Kennedy was shot?

Do you remember the Berlin Wall?

Is it Apartheid ending?

Is it the Challenger exploding?

Vietnam, the Persian Gulf, or Afghanistan?

9/11?

For some of you reading, the Berlin Wall was just a small section of required reading in your history class, for others it is a defining moment that solidified a generation. I shared the Berlin Wall in a workshop once. An older gentleman raised his hand

and asked, "When it went up, or when it came down?"

Major world events shape us.

Can you remember a world before 9/11?

Do you know much about the Cold War?

It may be difficult for us to connect with individuals who cannot remember these events, or the world before them.

Moreover, it can be nearly impossible to trust someone with our department, our budget, or our livelihood when they do not understand the impact of the Vietnam War or Watergate or trickle-down economics.

On the other side of the coin, for younger readers, these events seem like ancient history. Anyone who experienced them firsthand, then, may be just as ancient.

POP CULTURAL REFERENCES

What singers or artists do you remember from childhood and adolescence?

The Beatles

The Monkees

Sonny and Cher

Bon Jovi

Madonna

Michael Jackson

The Backstreet Boys

Green Day

Outkast

One Direction

Adele

The songs of our teens can quickly define our generation. The same can be said of TV shows, movies, and other pop cultural things. These pop culture references hold different weight than world events. We may not judge someone as harshly because they don't know the allure of a yellow submarine, or the *Thriller* Album, or who MGK is.

But there is subtle judgment.

This doesn't affect our confidence in their abilities as much as it discourages our belief in a connection.

We often feel we just don't, and won't ever, connect with these people.

TECHNOLOGY

What was the first piece of technology you remember wanting?

The answer to this question will immediately connect you with people who have a similar answer.

Some of us wanted a pager while others don't even know what that is.

Some of us wanted a party line for our room and others, a new iPhone.

Some of us were dying to own an Atari, N64 (*hello, Goldeneye*), or PS5.

Did you buy your music on vinyl? 8-track? Cassette? What about a CD, iPod, or simply stream it on your phone?

Since the turn of the twentieth century, the development of technology has exploded. Once we were an industrial society filled with blue-collar American stock, but through years of war, space exploration, and the invention of the internet, we are now a society filled with constant technological advancement. Necessity indeed was the mother of many inventions. NASA brought us Velcro, the insulin pump, solar cells, and Lasik surgery. War, and later the space race, brought us rockets, propulsion engines, and the internet. Now the technologies of the 1960s, '70s, '80s, and '90s give way to a new century and a gig economy.

The technology you remember wanting and using holds strong ties to who we are as people. It not only connects us with others in our generation but speaks to the socioeconomic status, geographic limitations, and social opportunities of your specific youth.

NOSTALGIA

When you grow up during the same time period as others, you have similar experiences during youth.

This is powerful.

Memories are powerful.

Nostalgia is powerful.

According to dictionary.com, nostalgia is "a sentimental longing or wistful affection for the past: typically for a period or place with happy personal associations."

These connections are deep and emotional.

According to Alan R. Hirsch in his report, "Nostalgia: A Neuropsychiatric Understanding,"[5] nostalgia is a yearning for an idealized past — "a longing for a sanitized impression of the past, what in psychoanalysis is referred to as a screen memory — not a true recreation of the past, but rather a combination of many different memories, all integrated together, and in the process all negative emotions filtered out."

Writer Lauren Martin puts it this way: "We put an emotional state within an era, or a specific frame, and choose to idealize that specific time. We deduce

---

[5] Alan R. Hirsch (1992), "Nostalgia: a Neuropsychiatric Understanding", in NA - Advances in Consumer Research Volume 19, eds. John F. Sherry, Jr. and Brian Sternthal, Provo, UT: Association for Consumer Research, Pages: 390-395.

that because we remember the feeling of happiness at the park, our childhood must have been better than right now. We even place it in inanimate objects, places and smells. Like with Horcruxes (shout-out to my *Harry Potter* fans), we lock away bits of ourselves into things and beings."[6]

In short, nostalgia is powerful.

If we lock away bits of ourselves into things and beings, it is incredibly edifying when people know and understand those things. When they don't know or understand the things from our past, they, in turn, don't understand us.

The point of all this is to reveal bias. We may not judge people according to the date on a calendar. But the details of our backgrounds, our shared history, and our nostalgia quotient often dictate our own unknown biases.

We must then look past our own biases and nostalgia to understand people individually.

WORLDVIEW

Worldview matters more than age.

Our interactions with major social events, pop culture, and technology work together to shape much of our worldview.

---

[6] https://www.elitedaily.com/life/science-behind-nostalgia-love-much/673184

This is why we can make *some* generalizations about people. People who share the same birth year no doubt share many of the same pop culture references, experienced the same world events, and used the same technologies.

But they don't share all of them.

Your individualized experience with these may skew your generational identity.

If you were raised by grandparents who watched *Nick-at-Night* and *Gunsmoke* every day, then you may identify older than you are.

If you lived in a smaller or rural area, you may have had less access to technology, and skew older.

Generations are helpful to understand broad similarities and differences among people.

We can use these tendencies for leadership decisions.

The values of Baby Boomers may be similar.

The worldview of Gen Z members may be similar.

When we understand this, it can help us create the cultural norms of our organizations.

But they are not the law.

When we understand this, it can help us create the cultural norms of our organizations.

But they are not the law. They are not the most important factors.

Individual truth always trumps generalized assumption.

WHERE TO START

There is a way forward. There are ways to train ourselves to understand our own tendencies and see the generational gaps more clearly.

More than that, there is a path of leadership so strong that it will actually bridge gaps between people of all generations, create collaboration where there is competition and establish appreciation where there is animosity.

The only way to do this is through keen self-awareness and continued learning.

There are four shifts in thinking that can serve as guides to growth as you read this book and consider your current practices.

1. We need to shift from unconscious to conscious.
2. We need to move from looking outward to looking inward.
3. We need to stop living in the past (or future) and start living in the present.
4. We need to change our default attitude from criticism and judgment to appreciation and gratitude.

The caveat, like all personal growth, is commitment.

These paradigm shifts take time and a willingness to learn.

We must work through our own insecurities to discover the powerful truths that people younger and older than us have to offer.

This is not a quick task. The ideas presented hereafter will offer no quick fixes.

We want to learn new things on the surface, but the commitment isn't always present. Some of us want to play the guitar like Eddie Van Halen (for my younger readers, he is a guitar player of mythic proportions from the 1980s) but we don't want to learn a chord.

We want to learn a new language, but we don't want to learn verb conjugations.

We want to become better leaders for multiple generations, but we do not want to take the time to learn what matters to them.

The problem with each of these scenarios is we desire to grow, but we don't discipline ourselves through the discomfort of growing pains.

These four paradigm-shifting ideas are the keys to humility we need to be a cross-generational leader.

We must learn them, apply them, and share them.

If you struggle to lead, you may think it is because of those you lead.

It probably isn't.

Younger or older, you likely work with people from other generations.

It is tempting to say people are just old and stuck in their ways, or too young and ridiculously naive.

Let's be clear: we do not have a generational problem. *We have a leadership problem.* What we call a generational gap is actually a lack of leadership and communication. Shifting our paradigm will enable us to cover the ground previously thought too wide of a chasm to cross. You can learn the skills you need to navigate cross-generational leadership in an ever-changing environment.

Entrepreneur, author, and award-winning speaker Jim Rohn said, "Managers help people see themselves as they are; Leaders help people to see themselves better than they are."

To equip others, today's leaders must first change their lens.

For too long, we've looked at older generations as a drain on our way of doing business while older leaders see young men and women in the workplace as entitled, lazy, and disinterested.

It's time we all look at ourselves.

CHAPTER 2.5: DIFFERENT IS GOOD

Thank You, John Adams

A quick note before we move forward.

With this discussion so far (as with most generations in the workforce discussions), we have focused primarily on generational differences.

It can be tempting to be frustrated by this.

The goal can appear to be uniformity.

As a leader, we can wish for everyone to have the same working values, styles, and preferences. It would make our jobs much simpler.

The goal is unity, not uniformity.

The problem isn't that different generations see the world differently.

Deep down, we want these differences.

Deep down, we *need* these differences.

We must acknowledge and navigate through these differences for the best outcome.

In a letter from the second President of the United States, John Adams, to his wife, Abigail Adams, dated May 12, 1780, he writes:

I must study Politicks and War so that my sons may have liberty to study Painting and Poetry Mathematicks and Philosophy. My sons ought to study Mathematics and Philosophy, Geography, natural History, Navel Architecture, navigation, Commerce and Agriculture, in order to give their children a right to study Painting, Poetry, Musick, Architecture, Statuary, Tapestry, and Porcelaine. [sic]

In President Adams' letter, we see a father's hopes for his children and his children's children. This two-generations-down vision is the approach we also want to take.

As leaders, we must account for those we leave behind.

We train, educate, and encourage upcoming generations to do more than we did.

If every generation viewed the world in the same way as its predecessor, there would be no progress.

Ironically, if younger generations see something differently than us, it means we probably did something right.

Younger generations too must not be so haughty as to believe their enlightenment is self-endowed.

We can run because they walked.

We stand on the shoulders of giants.

We build line upon line, precept upon precept.

We take what we understand, and we hope the next generation will push the boundaries of all we know to discover and invent more.

We wish for them what we never had.

We can breathe a sigh of relief when we realize *there's always a gap*.

Our job as leaders is to bridge that gap, not by making one generation like the other, but by calling out the strengths and talents of each group.

We build processes that value people.

We create the emotional and mental space to create our best work together.

We acknowledge generational differences from appreciation, not contempt.

CHAPTER 3: MAJOR TRENDS OF UPCOMING GENERATIONS

"Youth has no age."

- Pablo Picasso

Examining how each generation approaches different issues can give us a better understanding of communication style, how they gather information, how they value work, and what their approach to business is. For example:

How does each generation view work/life balance?

How do they view education?

How do they prefer to communicate?

Do they value productivity or affirmation?

Do they see themselves as team players, entrepreneurs, or participants?

Do they prefer more autonomy or direction in their work?

While there are no universal answers to the above questions, we have discovered some trends among upcoming generations. We will look at each trend and a corresponding lesson to be considered.

TREND #1: EMERGING ADULTHOOD

It seems that adolescence — that period before we become adults — is growing longer. In *The Age of Opportunity*, Laurence Steinberg makes the case that human beings are entering and staying in adolescence longer than ever before. This special phase in human development is starting earlier and lasting longer.

Steinberg defines adolescence as "the stage of development that begins with puberty and ends with economic and social independence." Based on his research, it is beginning as early as the age of 10 and continues well into a person's 20s. Which goes a long way to explain why your new recruits are working at the office and going home to their parents' house at the end of the day.

This concept of extended adolescence is not new. It was first made famous by psychologist Erik Erikson, who, in his theory on the different stages of human development, termed this stage a "psychosocial moratorium." Yet many child psychologists believe today's children seem to be idling in this hiatus period more so than ever before. "I'm keenly aware of the shift, as I often see adolescents presenting with some of the same complaints as college graduates," says Columbia

University psychiatrist Mirjana Domakonda, who was not involved in the new study. "Twenty-five is the new 18, and delayed adolescence is no longer a theory, but a reality. In some ways, we're all in a 'psychosocial moratorium' experimenting with a society where swipes constitute dating and likes are the equivalent of conversation."[7]

As you can see, this idea has a few different names.

It has been called "psychosocial moratorium", "extended adolescence", and even "permanent adolescence."

Yikes! Permanent adolescence seems a bit harsh. I prefer emerging adulthood.

Especially regarding young adults in the workforce.

When *does* someone become an adult?

Every culture in the history of mankind has answered this question.

From Bar and Bat Mitzvah, to Rumspringa, to Hamar Cow Jumping,[8] various cultures across the globe welcome children into adulthood through various means.

In American culture, however, the answer is less direct.

---

https://www.scientificamerican.com/article/extended-adolescence-when-25-is-the-new-181/

[8] https://www.globalcitizen.org/en/content/13-amazing-coming-of-age-traditions-from-around-th/

We are the melting pot, so what is our specific call to adulthood?

Historically, there are five rites of passage which apply to every American generation. These are, no doubt, debatable. But, over the last 100 years or so, achieving some combination of these five was your step into adulthood.

- Graduate (something, anything — high school or college)
- Get married
- Have children
- Get a job (begin your career)
- Buy a house

We have no official rites of passage as a culture, but our subconscious ideas of what it means to be an adult haven't changed that much. It was the same for me as my grandparents.

The difference is pace.

My grandparents achieved all five in a week!

Okay, a year, but it was fast. Really fast.

They graduated high school on a Friday.

Ran off and got married that weekend.

On Monday my PawPaw went to work, and nine months later my Uncle Johnny was born.

Today, the average marriage age is 32 years old, according to the WeddingWire Newlywed Report. Just 12 years ago, the average couple got married at age 27, and according to demographic data from the U.S. Census Bureau, the average marriage ages for men and women were 22.9 and 20.3 in 1950 — not even 75 years ago![9]

What it means to be an adult has changed.

What it means to transition from childhood to adulthood has changed.

Being a child may have its trouble, but adulting is hard.

LESSON #1: ADULTING IS HARD

The threshold from childhood into adulthood was more obvious in years past.

It was much clearer 100, 50, or even 30 years ago.

You stepped into adulthood in much more explicit ways, and much earlier ages.

Now, that transition takes years.

So much so that we have the verb *adulting*.

I don't have to be an adult all the time, I can adult at different times.

Adulting, as a verb, reveals that adulthood is an emerging process.

At work, I can be head of my department, while at home I don't do my own laundry.

---

[9] weddingwire.com

At work, I can oversee a multi-million-dollar project, but share a family phone plan.

At work, I enroll and oversee healthcare benefits, while staying on my mom and dad's plan.

None of this, by the way, is judgmental.

Nothing I have written, so far, has a value statement attached.

If you feel yourself being judgmental, that may reveal some of your bias.

It simply means our cultural norms are shifting.

Our definitions haven't caught up.

Psychologist Mirjana Domakonda feels that instead of pushing young adults to mature faster, we should embrace the cultural shift and develop ways to both meet the psychological needs of modern teens while also setting them up for future success. Domakonda suggests one such strategy might be expanding mental health services for adolescents, particularly because 75 percent of major mental illnesses emerge by the mid-20s. She also feels we should stop arbitrarily defining 18 as the age of adulthood and recognize that psychosocial development occurs differently in different people. "Researchers need to recognize that emerging adults are a unique developmental cohort and stop lumping them in the 18- to 65-year-old category for studies of adults," she says. "That will help us learn about their specific needs so we may develop targeted prevention and treatment strategies [for mental illness]."[10]

As leaders, we can no longer arbitrarily assign adulthood to an age — or even a stage of life — as clearly as we once did.

Nor can we assign our own assumptions that go with it.

Now we must gauge each person individually.

We must focus on roles, needs, and immediate expectations rather than a collective expression of what we think adulthood is.

Adulting, it seems, really is hard.

TREND #2: DIGITAL NATIVITY

My son Everett was born in 2018. He is a digital native. My phone is an unorganized mess of apps. There is no rhyme or reason to the order of the icons. I do not put things into folders and as I add new ones, they get tacked into the mess. Sometimes I have to go to the App Store to search for an app I already have on my phone but cannot find. Not so for Everett.

Since he was 18-months old, he has navigated my phone better than I. He knows that two swipes to the

---

[10] https://www.scientificamerican.com/article/extended-adolescence-when-25-is-the-new-181/

left will take him to Disney+. Another swipe left and in the right corner is Netflix.

He can find his own cartoon.

He can unlock my phone.

He can turn on the Smart TV and locate multiple apps.

He is a digital native.

Not me.

I am a digital immigrant born in a distant land called the eighties.

I remember wires and plugging things in.

Our remote control was me.

Our entertainment didn't come from a handheld video screen.

When I grew up, a vacation was visiting relatives who lived far away.

Traveling back then was much different than it is today. Yes, for all you younger readers, we still had cars, but we didn't have phones or tablets to distract us kids.

No, we played games.

Road trip games.

Games like Billboard Alphabet, or License Plate Round Up, or Spot All the Red Cars.

We would get rowdy and begin fighting over who called that last red sports car, and Mom would join in with her favorite game, Imaginary Line.

"There is an imaginary line between you and your brother. DO NOT CROSS IT!"

Of course, we crossed it.

Then Dad joined in the vacation fun with his favorite game, Turn Around.

"Stop all that now, or I will turn this car around!"

Traveling just looked different back then. Ahh, the good ole days.

I still love vacations.

Our kids still sit in the backseat, but they aren't yelling and fighting like I did.

There is glorious silence.

Because of gadgets.

Digital natives in their natural habitat.

With the advent of handheld devices, child-friendly entertainment, and excellent data plans, our kids can make longer trips than we could with less fuss.

But at what cost?

LESSON #2: DOPAMINE IS A BIG DEAL.

"I feel tremendous guilt," admitted Chamath Palihapitiya, former Vice President of User Growth at Facebook, to an audience of Stanford students. He was responding to a question about his involvement in exploiting consumer behavior. "The short-term, dopamine-driven feedback loops that we have created are destroying how society works," he explained. In Palihapitiya's talk, he highlighted something most of us know but few really appreciate: smartphones and the social media platforms they support are turning us into *bona fide* addicts. While it's easy to dismiss this claim as hyperbole, platforms like Facebook, Snapchat, and Instagram leverage the very same neural circuitry used by slot machines and cocaine to keep us using their products as much as possible.[11]

According to a "Harvard University — Science in the News" article written by Trevor Haynes, our bodies crave dopamine. Dopamine is a chemical produced by our brains that plays a starring role in motivating behavior. It gets released when we take a bite of delicious food, when we have sex, after we exercise, and, importantly, when we have successful social interactions. In an evolutionary context, it rewards us for beneficial behaviors and motivates us to repeat them. If we do not get enough dopamine-

---

[11] https://www.youtube.com/watch?v=PMotykw0SIk

producing social interactions in typical ways, then we look for unhealthy ways to produce dopamine.[12]

If we aren't getting regular doses of it through real life experiences, we turn to devices and the social media platforms they support to get our fix. Upcoming generations are growing up on this cycle, and it is changing the way social and work interactions happen.

A client of mine became frustrated when she saw productivity decline. As we walked by the cubicles of employees, she pointed out employee after employee on their phone. When I asked more questions, I found her frustration rooted in her older, more phone-free lifestyle in combat with her team's behaviors. She wanted her employees to lay down their phones and do more work. This is a reasonable request — after all, employers pay us to do work, not check social media, play games, or text our friends. I asked a series of questions that changed her perspective and created room for her to adjust her leadership style.

The main one was: "Have you ever worked with an addict before?"

---

[12] https://sitn.hms.harvard.edu/flash/2018/dopamine-smartphones-battle-time/

ARE WE REALLY ADDICTS?

Many social media apps take advantage of the dopamine-driven learning strategy. Similar to slot machines, many apps implement a reward pattern optimized to keep you engaged as much as possible. Variable reward schedules were introduced by psychologist B.F. Skinner in the 1930s. In his experiments, he found that mice respond most frequently to reward-associated stimuli when the reward was administered after a varying number of responses, precluding the animal's ability to predict when they would be rewarded. Humans are no different; if we perceive a reward to be delivered at random, and if checking for the reward comes at little cost, we end up checking habitually (e.g., gambling addiction). If you pay attention, you might find yourself checking your phone at the slightest feeling of boredom, purely out of habit. Programmers work very hard behind the screens to keep you doing exactly that.[13]

For many, addiction to devices is a struggle.

The dopamine-smartphone feedback loop is a measurable cycle in which many people —across multiple generations — find themselves caught in.

When we see people around us as addicts, we can change our perspective.

---

[13] https://sitn.hms.harvard.edu/flash/2018/dopamine-smartphones-battle-time/

The cycle of addiction is something many of us understand and sympathize.

Smokers are addicted to cigarettes.

No matter how you feel about smoking, you (probably) understand the physical and mental addictions that chain people to the habit.

Phones are also a habit.

Most mobile phone users check their phones up to 63 times daily.

Americans spend an average screen time of 5.4 hours on their mobile phones daily.

In 2018, there were 294.15 million smartphone users in America. That number is growing every day.

Social media is responsible for 2 hours and 24 minutes of global internet time spent online by an average user daily.[14]

How do *you* view phones?

Are they a nuisance?

Are they a distraction?

Are they a tool?

When we change our verbiage, we can change our perspective.

---

[14] https://techjury.net/blog/how-much-time-does-the-average-american-spend-on-their-phone/#gref

When we look for the win-win, we begin to build a culture within our companies that strengthens everyone's position. The company gets the productivity it needs and deserves, and the employees get the compassion they need as they learn to change their habits.

If phones are tools, we can learn to use them more efficiently.

We all use our phones for work. But we don't always use them for work *at* work.

Instead of hoping people will operate with integrity and use their phone appropriately, we should discuss the issue and solve problems collectively.

My advice is: don't fight it, *use it*.

Use it as a point of collaboration.

Use it to find work life balance.

Use the conversation to open up other conversations.

Phones are not going away, so we must adjust.

The point is not to give in to something — the point is to make your current circumstances work for you and not against you. That is what a good leader does, *and you are a good leader.* Shift your paradigm and lead from a perspective of concern, compassion, and mutual benefit.

The smoke break may begat the phone break.

TREND #3: INSTANT GRATIFICATION

This is a big one.

The trend of instant gratification is the most relevant when discussing generational gaps with upcoming generations. While this trend cannot be assigned to every individual within a generation, the idea of instant gratification cannot be overstated. Almost all of Gen Z and most Millennials have practically never waited for anything in their life.

I remember waiting.

Do you remember how long we had wait to watch a movie?

First, it released in theaters.

If you missed it, you waited a year for it to arrive at your local Blockbuster to rent.

Then you had to wait another month for it to be moved from the "new release" section because your dad wouldn't pay the extra dollar!

Now we can watch the latest Marvel movie on our phone while it's in theaters.

Food delivery has changed.

When I was growing up, the only place that delivered was the pizza place.

Now we have Uber Eats, DoorDash, and tons of other services that can bring you a snack or meal from any nearby restaurant, whether the restaurant delivers or not.

Amazon has 2-day delivery, same-day delivery, and even predictive delivery *(this doesn't actually exist yet, but mark my words)*.

I remember when Saturday mornings used to mean something.

It was a day with no school, plenty of cereal, and lots of cartoons.

Cartoons were on television from seven in the morning until noon.

Now my kids can watch cartoons anytime across multiple platforms.

Saturday mornings are meaningless to them.

Is there *nothing* sacred anymore???

I digress.

The fact of the matter is we know what we want, and we want it now.

Not just upcoming generations, but all of us.

Who among us has not closed a video when it took longer than 10 seconds to load?

Let he who is without sin cast the first phone.

As a society, we are losing our ability to pay attention.

According to research, our attention span has markedly decreased in just 15 years. In 2000, it was

12 seconds. Now, 15 years later, it's shrunk significantly to 8.25 seconds.[15]

LESSON #3: MILLENNIALS AREN'T ENTITLED

We think Millennials and Gen Zers are entitled.

We have been throwing around this label for years.

We believe this because we've trained one another to believe it.

The news has said it, articles have said it, and my neighbor has said it.

There is a more profound truth here in their behavior which we gloss over.

According to lexico.com "entitled" means, "Believing oneself to be inherently deserving of privileges or special treatment." I've worked with thousands of young people.

I do not believe they feel this way.

They definitely want things, sooner than later, but they are not privileged or entitled. They know they must work.

They believe in the value of productive work.

---

[15] National Center for Biotechnology Information, U.S. National Library of Medicine, Associated Press

Upcoming generations are not entitled — they are impatient.

When you put together emerging adulthood, dopamine cycles, and instant gratification, the sum of its parts is impatience.

Upcoming generations are able to hack their way through life.

They are capable, smart, and willing to produce.

They are online more than they are offline. They want to do things.

They want to succeed, but they see no need for seniority or tenure.

In the mind of a young person, if they know how to do something, why should they go through a six-month class to pass a test proving they know the material?

Instead, why not just test into a job or a skill and market that skill?

We must move away from the archaic language of entitlement and move toward more open, responsive language of impatience.

Then we can begin to give opportunities fairly and frequently.

If time isn't an issue, we should not make it an issue.

CHAPTER 4: THREE COMMON BIASES OF ESTABLISHED GENERATIONS

"You can't help getting older. But you don't have to get old."

- George Burns

When do you become old?

"You're only as old as you feel."

"You're as old as you think you are."

"Age is just a number."

"Old is always twenty years from now."

Maybe you ascribe to one of the maxims above.

AARP magazine reports that perceptions of the onset of old age vary widely among different generations. Millennials, for example, say that you are old once you turn 59. Gen Xers, on the other hand, hold a slightly more generous view, saying that old age begins at 65. When it comes to boomers and the silent generation, both agree that you're not really old until you hit age 73.[16]

AARP also asked the question: "What age do you consider to be old?" Individuals in upcoming generations were also asked to show what "old" looks like. Then participants were introduced to some real "old" people of that age in the #DisruptAging campaign.

Old really is relative.

There are many definitions with no specific age.

I have always said, "You get old when your mind gets closed."

In this chapter, we will discuss three common biases of established generations.

While the following biases are not a sign that you are old, they may be a warning.

DECLINISM

No matter what your age, someone older than you said, "Things were better in the old days" or "When I was growing up…" or maybe, "This world is going to hell in a hand basket" or some such equivalent. If we're honest, we may be the one saying these things.

---

[16] https://www.aarp.org/home-family/friends-family/info-2017/what-age-are-you-old-fd.html

The idea that the world, society, or nation will never be as good in the future as it was in the past is called declinism. With declinism, we remember the past as better than it was. We also expect the future to be worse than it probably will be. This defeatist attitude is prevalent in business as well as politics and social theory. We hear this kind of speech or have these kinds of thoughts internally as we work with people who are younger, less experienced, or have a different worldview than we do.

Jesse Richardson describes current declinism rather poetically: "Despite living in the most peaceful and prosperous time in history, many people believe things are getting worse. The 24-hour news cycle, with its reporting of overtly negative and violent events, may account for some of this effect. We can also look to the generally optimistic view of the future in the early 20th century as being shifted to a dystopian and apocalyptic expectation after the world wars, and during the cold war. The greatest tragedy of this bias may be that our collective expectation of decline may contribute to a real-world self-fulfilling prophecy."[17]

CURSE OF KNOWLEDGE

The "curse of knowledge", or "the curse of expertise", is a cognitive bias where we incorrectly assume that everyone knows as much as we do on a

---

[17] https://yourbias.is/declinism

given topic. When we know something, it can be hard to imagine what it would be like not knowing that piece of information. In turn, this makes it difficult to share our knowledge, because we struggle to understand the other party's state of mind.[18]

Once we understand something, we think it is obvious to everyone.

Chip and Dan Heath write, "Lots of us have expertise in particular areas. Becoming an expert in something means that we become more and more fascinated by nuance and complexity. That's when the curse of knowledge kicks in, and we start to forget what it's like not to know what we know."[19]

Because of this bias more experienced employees, managers, and leaders find it difficult to empathize with someone who does not have the same knowledge.

We simply forget what we didn't know when we were younger.

The disappointing truth about this bias is how difficult it is to recognize.

Many of us fall prey to this curse of knowledge with our realizing it.

---

[18] https://thedecisionlab.com/reference-guide/management/curse-of-knowledge/
[19] Chip and Dan Heath, authors of *Made to Stick: Why Some Ideas Survive and Others Die*

Right now, most readers assume they have avoided this curse.

We are patient with younger, lesser experienced team members.

We are good teachers and help people to understand.

We are empathic, and quick to assist people.

Maybe.

In the workplace, this bias can be elusive, so think of a more practical example: the flat tire.

Ever ask a younger person to help you change a tire?

Or gotten a call from your twenty-something asking *how* to change a tire?

It is absolutely, ridiculously unbelievable, how many young people don't know the first thing about changing a tire.

It's all the time they spend on phones.

What are they even teaching in school these days???

However, this is not a skill we are born knowing.

There was a time when you and I didn't know how to change a tire.

Moreover, this skill has nothing to do with age.

If we could somehow zap Alexander the Great, or George Washington, or Joan of Arc here today, they would have no clue how to change a tire.

Why? Lack of experience.

It's the same for our younger workforce.

It probably isn't a skill we learned without someone guiding us through it, but we can become incredulous when we hear someone doesn't know how. We've forgotten what it was like to be the novice. We've lost connection with compassion for those younger than us and let frustration and assumption fill the narrative.

We lose patience quickly when people can't change a tire.

We also lose patience when we think they *ought* to know something.

What implications can "Curse of Knowledge Bias" have in our workplace?

THE CURSE AND THE CURE

This bias can lead to communication gaps, empathy gaps, and, ultimately, decreased retention rates. Communication gaps go beyond cross-generational differences. The curse of knowledge is often revealed in our frequently used jargon, acronyms, and shorthand. The longer we have been included with a particular industry, company, or field of study, the more we forget how often we use abbreviated language.

Empathy gaps can leave people feeling undervalued at work.

Study after study reveals that being valued or appreciated at work is more and more important in today's workforce.

The Great Place to Work Trust Index found employee recognition was most important to 37% of employees. Teams scoring in the top 20% of engagement experience 59% fewer turnovers. Only approximately 34% of U.S. workers feel engaged.[20]

Many managers in leadership think younger generations are too coddled.

When we hear statements and statistics like the ones above, we can be left confused.

"Are we supposed to go around saying 'good job' all the time?"

"Are we supposed to celebrate people for just showing up?"

"How do I make people feel more valued at their job? Just do your job."

Instead of thinking of valuing people's work as merely praise, or overt praise, consider the curse of knowledge.

When we are guilty of the curse of knowledge, we can create communication and empathy gaps. We can patronize people. We can undermine their position unintentionally with our nonverbal cues

---

[20] https://www.greatplacetowork.com/resources/blog/creating-a-culture-of-recognition

and verbal condescension. This makes people feel less valued. Why?

We literally value them less because we judge them for their lack of knowledge.

This subtle belief is stronger than we think.

This hidden judgement is more obvious than we know.

When we think people are children, we tend to treat them like children.

They don't appreciate it.

So, they leave.

THE FUNDAMENTAL ATTRIBUTION ERROR

The fundamental attribution error (also known as correspondence bias or over-attribution effect) is the tendency for people to over-emphasize dispositional, or personality-based explanations, for behaviors observed in others while at the same time under-emphasizing situational explanations.

In other words, people have a cognitive bias to assume that a person's actions depend on what "kind" of person that person is rather than on the social and environmental forces that influence the person.[21]

We see the fundamental attribution error all around us.

Many stereotypes can arise from this bias.

It is also the explanation why first impressions matter, or why we will never give certain individuals the benefit of the doubt.

We judge others by their actions and judge ourselves by our intentions.

In other words, we tend to cut ourselves a break and hold others more accountable.

As we become more established in our careers, we can find it hard to allow for situational hardships for others. If you have ever chastised someone for being late, while making a reasonable excuse for your tardiness later, you have made a fundamental attribution error.

This can be especially evident in cross-generational leadership. We often associate a team member's mistake with their age rather than circumstance. We can then carry this over to others of the same age as a stereotype.

---

[21] https://www.simplypsychology.org/fundamental-attribution.html

OVERCOMING BIAS

While many of these biases are deeply rooted and may be impossible to completely overcome, we can get better. Declinism, the curse of knowledge, and the fundamental attribution error can all be present in our lives without us even knowing it. So, how do we overcome?

1. Self-Awareness

Self-awareness may be the all-time greater "chicken or egg" scenario in leadership development. How do you *become* self-aware?

For the purposes of these biases, just assume you are guilty.

Be tough on yourself and ask your team if you have demonstrated any of these traits.

2. Practice Gratitude

There are thousands of writings on gratitude that are much more complete and helpful than anything I could write here.

So, read a gratitude book. Keep a gratitude journal. Mediate.

Whatever your chosen gratitude, practice. Practice it.

Gratitude is the gateway to humility.

Humility is the antidote for bias.

3. Self-Regulation

Self-regulation is the ability to manage your emotions and behaviors in accordance with the needs of the situation.

Good leaders are great self-regulators.

They think before they act.

Self-regulators tend to act in accordance with their values, see the good in others, and remain flexible in stressful situations.

PART 2

BEST PRACTICES OF CROSS-
GENERATIONAL LEADERS

CHAPTER 5: THE PROBLEM WITH COMMON SENSE

"I do not think much of ages. People are people. What does it matter how old or young they are? It is a category, and I do not like categories. It is a sort of pigeonhole or a label."

- Louis L'Amour

The remedy for many of the unconscious biases discussed in the previous chapter could simply be common sense.

If people from other generations (often younger generations) just had common sense, they would not be so quick to judge their lack of knowledge, give false attributions, or believe the dismal wave of decline.

But common sense is not as common as we think.

The trouble is the way we interpret the phrase *common sense.*

We often focus on the noun "sense." As in, "you need more sense."

The *perceived* problem with many young people is that they don't have the sense to make the right decisions.

We should focus less on the noun, "sense", and more on the adjective, "common."

For common sense to work, it has to, in fact, be common.

It must be shared.

Common sense generally refers to the most obvious course of action or the decision most often made. One definition reads "sound and prudent judgment based on a simple perception of the situation or facts."[22]

But who is to say what defines "sound and prudent?"

For one group of people, a course of action may be obvious, while for others it may be a mystery. For one person the obvious course of action may be up, and for another person the obvious course of action may be down.

If common sense is making the most obvious decision, what makes a decision obvious? The answer: values.

---

[22] https://www.merriam-webster.com/dictionary/common%20sense

We make decisions based on values.

For the most obvious decision to be agreed upon, we must share the same values.

Common sense equals common values.

When we don't share the same values as others, we make different decisions than those individuals.

We interpret this as a lack of common sense on *their* part.

This is where the problem starts.

The problem escalates when we assume people share our personal values.

ASSUMPTIONS

We must break through our own assumptions as cross-generational leaders.

If you want to be a better leader, work to understand the personal values of others.

Personal values are the things that are important to us.

They are the characteristics, traits, or ideas that guide our decisions and motivate our actions.

Understanding your peers', employees', and supervisors' personal values greatly impacts your influence.

The first step in this process is to assume you don't know their values.

Certainly, do not assume you have the same values.

Break through the assumption.

At first glance, we can think this is simple. We don't assume people have the same personal values.

On the deepest levels, this is often true.

We can quickly accept that what is most important in your life is probably different than mine.

Many of us are adept in at least considering someone's religion, marital status, parental status, sexual orientation, and other major life factors in accordance with their values.

The assumptions we make are much more subtle.

It isn't major life components that create division and a lack of "common sense." It is the gradual changes that have occurred over decades that produce varying generational value systems. Furthermore, it's the understanding and application of these generational values that are often misaligned.

Take courtesy, for example. Who doesn't value courtesy?

That depends.

What is the interpretation of the word?

I grew up in rural Oklahoma, and the personal value instilled in me was to call everyone "ma'am."

While some people might appreciate this, others find it offensive.

My mama thinks it is courtesy.

Our new middle-aged human resources director thinks it is rude.

Even if we agree that courtesy is a shared value, what about when it comes in conflict with another workplace value of efficiency?

What is more important? Courtesy, or efficiency?

You can't say both. Both may be important, but which one is more important? As a good leader should I say "hello" to everyone even if it is entirely inefficient of our time? How courteous should I be?

How about the value of honesty? Surely we can all agree that "honesty is the best policy."

Maybe. But do we really want everyone being completely honest with everyone all the time?

Like, no filter honesty. Like, brutal honesty.

Probably not. We all have different personal values.

We cannot assume we share the same values.

As our population has grown, access to information has increased and connectivity with a more diverse swath of individuals has risen, while our shared values has declined.

It makes sense that when we all used to watch the same three TV channels that our values were more similar.

When we only connected with people in geographic proximity, we tended to share the same values.

When we received news and information from limited sources, our value systems migrated very little.

That is no longer the case.

Instead, we have a multigenerational workforce with multifaceted beliefs and values.

These personal values systems are too unique and nuanced for leaders to assume we understand each other inherently or subconsciously.

We must break through the assumption.

THE HUMAN BEHAVIORAL TRIANGLE

A few years ago, I found myself running into my own assumptions.

As founder and CEO of Paradigm Shift, I found myself in conflict with my team more frequently than I would like.

All conflict comes from unmet expectations.

If we are to be better leaders, we should seek to reduce conflict by clarifying expectations.

We work through our own assumptions to identify and understand the beliefs, feelings, and values of others.

We created the Human Behavioral Triangle as a tool to help do just that.

It began as an internal device for us to use in performance reviews and corrective conversations. We have since taught it to thousands of leaders across the country to increase clarity and reduce conflict.

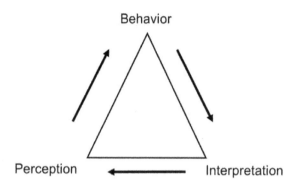

The Human Behavioral Triangle illustrates the relationship between our behaviors, interpretations, and perceptions.

We exhibit a behavior.

Others interpret that behavior.

They build perceptions from that interpretation.

That perception, in turn, shapes their behavior.

The way we perceive situations (correct or not) shapes our actions, and the cycle starts again. We follow this pattern no matter who we are. We do it unconsciously. Without fail, others perform the same behavioral triangle. It is human nature.

Our offices are more than four walls, random desks, and meeting rooms. They are also people. There are different races, religions, personal habits, educational levels, genders, orientations, creeds, traumas, and other factors that inform people's own personal values systems.

These value systems guide our behaviors.

They also create the lens by which we interpret others' behaviors.

Each arrow in the Human Behavioral Triangle is an opportunity for assumption.

This feeds the generational gap. (Truthfully, it feeds all our differences and areas of conflict.)

Instead of allowing the triangular cycle to continue undeterred, we can use this as a tool for conversation when we disagree or aren't functioning at our highest levels.

We often assume people are lazy or entitled, or out of touch and judgmental.

These assumptions build perceptions that fuel division.

Perception isn't reality. But perception dictates behavior.

Several years ago, my team believed I was untouchable and not to be bothered.

I would frequently hear of problems much later than a leader should or opportunities were unshared because the team felt I would not care to hear about them.

This wasn't the case, so how did this belief begin?

Texting. Rather, the lack thereof.

I am admittedly old school. I use my phone for everything, but have no problem putting it down. When I am in a meeting or with my family, I will disregard my phone entirely.

Our workforce (many Gen Z) would text me and I would not reply quickly. I would eventually reply — an hour later, or later that night, or even the next day *(God forbid, I know).*

The team began to believe that I just didn't care since I wasn't quick to respond.

Behavior: delayed texting

Interpretation: That isn't important to Jerrod.

Perception: Jerrod gets annoyed with texts.

New Behavior: Don't text Jerrod.

This wasn't the case. In fact, I wanted to know what was going on. My personal value of family time and in-person interactions was in conflict with my team.

Neither of us were wrong, by the way.

We just have different values.

To me, it is rude to check my phone in person.

To my team, it is understandable and acceptable.

We used the Behavior Triangle to understand the conflict and clarify expectations.

They now know that I will eventually respond. If I am too slow, they can nudge me with another text. That's totally fine.

I now work to respond more quickly. That was a fair request.

I also use notifications, especially when away from my phone.

As leaders, we have the opportunity to discuss our perceptions to better understand our team's behaviors. We should not ignore it.

We absolutely should not base our actions on assumptions.

FULL-VALUE CONTRACTS

Do you view yourself as a leader?

You should.

We have used that term throughout the book and will continue to do so.

You may dismiss the term and think of other people in leadership positions with more authority.

But do not let your age or position disqualify you as a leader.

You are neither too young nor too old.

Positions do not define leaders.

Leaders define the position.

You are a leader.

John Maxwell said, "Leadership is influence. Nothing more. Nothing less."

For the purpose of this book, a leader is anyone who has influence, and you have influence.

How much? That varies widely.

Our level of influence is fluid. It can lessen and it can increase.

Every interaction you have is an opportunity to build influence.

Leadership is influence.

Influence is built on trust.

Trust is grown from relationship.

Relationships are born in connections.

One of the most obvious ways to build unity amongst your team is to discuss it.

Openly discussing, not only your core values, but also your daily interactions and how they affect others. The Human Behavioral Triangle is an incredible tool for these sometimes-difficult discussions.

If there are divisions, conflict, or frustrations, don't ignore them.

As a leader, you have an opportunity to bust divisive assumptions before they take root by creating a full-value contract. Full-value contracts form from a desire to fully value all the members of the group.

A full-value contract is establishing social norms and acceptable behaviors within a group so everyone in the group feels fully valued. We all operate under spoken and unspoken norms every day of our lives. These norms are social agreements that we have chosen to abide by. The social agreements change in different settings with different people.

How we act at a football game versus a hospital, for example.

How two friends interact versus adding a third friend, or a newcomer, to the group.

A full-value contract acknowledges these norms openly and addresses how we can do better.

My good friend Mark Collard, experiential education expert, describes a full-value contract as a device consisting of a set of behavioral norms that help individuals and groups achieve their program goals in a safe and supportive environment.[23]

He further describes full-value contracts as accomplishing three broad tasks:

---

[23] Mark Collard is one of the world's greatest facilitators. Check out my good friend's incredible work on FVC at https://www.playmeo.com/full-value/

1. Understand and create safe behavioral norms under which the group will operate.
2. Seek a commitment to adhere to these norms by everyone in the group.
3. Accept a shared responsibility for the maintenance of the group.

Within a business, a leader can implement full-value contracts and change the entire dynamic by which we operate. A full-value contract is a starting point for any group. It provides the ground rules for behavior, which in turn fuels the communication of the group. A full-value contract can be between two people or hundreds. It is never too late to create one, and it is a resource you can use to dissolve tension amongst peers. There are some absolutely fantastic resources on creating full-value contracts. Check out Mark Collard's site, playmeo.com, or visit PS.company as good starting points.

The premise of "common sense" is based upon a misconstrued perception — that we all have enough in common to think, process, and decide the same thing in any given set of circumstances, thus achieving a common outcome.

This idea fuels the generation gap as we typically see it.

What is common to you is not common to them. We have young people in the workforce with less in common with us — therefore, they may not handle each situation the same way you would. Conversely, as a young person, you may not understand why your older counterparts make the decisions they make. This lack of commonality can lead to more than a typical gap.

If left unchecked, it can lead to a complete breakdown in morale and authority for you as a leader.

Fully value team members.

Break through the assumptions.

Build the common sense together.

CHAPTER 6: COMMUNICATION

"The art of communication is the language of leadership."

- James Humes

Gilbert Amelio, President and CEO of National Semiconductor Corporation, said, "Developing excellent communication skills is absolutely essential to effective leadership. The leader must be able to share knowledge and ideas to transmit a sense of urgency and enthusiasm to others. If a leader can't get a message across clearly and motivate others to act on it, then having a message doesn't even matter."

Good leaders communicate well.

This is a timeless truth.

The way we communicate, however, is not so timeless.

Communication isn't just verbal and nonverbal anymore.

It isn't just the written word versus the spoken word with which leaders must contend.

If you research types of communication, there are all sorts of interpretations.

Seriously, I Googled "methods of communication" and got:

- The 5 methods of communication
- The 7 methods of communication
- The 6 methods of communication
- The 10 methods of communication
- The 4 methods of communication

How many methods of communication are there?

There is verbal communication, written communication, oral communication (what's the difference between that and verbal???), face-to-face, nonverbal, visual, and more.

The list seems to never stop.

Furthermore, the delivery mechanisms seem endless.

Do we need to have a meeting?

Will a Zoom call do?

Or do they use Microsoft Teams? Google Hangouts? FaceTime?

Does Skype still exist?

Should I email that? *(No, they will never see it.)*

Do I send a text message? Maybe that's too personal.

How many emojis are too many? I want this to be friendly, but still professional.

Can we use social media for this message? Is it professional to Snapchat?

Wait, that doesn't seem right. Forget that question.

I will just send a Slack message. You may, or may not, know Slack.

By the time you read this, Slack may or may not be in vogue or even in business.

Either way, the message here is clear (see what I did there):

Communication changes quickly.

Cross-generational leaders understand the importance of communication.

They strive to be mindful of what they are saying, how they are saying it, and the methods by which they are saying it. Because mistakes can happen...[24]

---

[24] https://www.freemake.com/blog/12-funny-autocorrect-mistakes/
https://www.buzzfeednews.com/article/jessicamisener/the-30-most-hilarious-autocorrect-struggles-ever

Are you doing the Nutcracker this year?

Yep! I'm auctioning kids tomorrow.

Suctioning kids.

Ridiculous auto cat rectal

Birdseed!

I AM AUDITIONING KIDS FORPLAY

Wow I am sorry I asked! Hahahahah

I heard mom got stung by a few bees this morning. Is she ok??? Hospital???

She is okay now. No hospital.

She had to take the deep penis.

Uh...what?

Read 10:45 PM

I had to inject her with an EPIC PENIS.

Oh for Christ's sake.

Epi Pen

83

Are you done painting Jason's living room yet?

Yeah just finished

What color is it again?

It's called period red

Dude. No. You're sick.

Holy shit. It's called Persian red. I got autocorrected. EPIC FAIL!

Omgggg we are dying here

Can't wait to see you babe! Hurry up and get here!

Whoo hoo! It's Friday. Screw the gym! I'm getting pregnant tonight!

Uh...shouldn't we talk about that first?

HAHAHAHA Oh my god.

I wrote Pringles and it autocorrected to pregnant.

I almost had a heart attack

Happy Birthday to you!
Happy Birthday to you!
Happy Birthday dead husband!
Happy Birthday to you!

Thanks. I assume you meant "dear".

Ahhhhh

Yes!!! I mean that is crazy autocorrect! Sorry babe.

MINDFUL COMMUNICATION

I chose the word "mindful" to describe communication for a particular purpose.

To be mindful is to be conscious or aware of something.

We should be mindful of our communication style.

In writing this, it is difficult to give specific advice for how to communicate more effectively.

With all the conversation thus far on personal value systems, cultural norms, and generational differences, there will be no one-size-fits-all answers here.

I don't believe there are correct answers to how you should communicate.

I don't believe there is a "do and do not" list.

There may not even be helpful suggestions because every generational circumstance is unique, and your work environment is completely unique.

Mindful, I believe, is the most appropriate encouragement for healthy communication across generations. Mindful communication considers three elements: speed, medium, and message.

SPEED

The speed of the response is directly related to the significance of the relationship.

It isn't just the message that matters. It's who sent it.

How important someone is to us is often reflected in how quickly we respond to them.

If my wife calls me, I call back immediately, if not sooner.

If a telemarketer calls, I never call back.

Everyone else falls somewhere in between.

We should be mindful, then, how quickly we respond to our team.

I shared earlier that I have been guilty of responding too slowly.

Older audiences remember what it was like to only have a landline and be unreachable. This tends to create more grace on the response time.

In general, the younger the audience, the more quickly they expect a response.

This is important, because, remember, all conflict comes from unmet expectations.

As leaders, we must be mindful of what our communication says.

The speed at which we reply is conveying potentially unintended messages.

We should try to meet our teammates on their turf when we can.

We should also clearly communicate our expectations and intentions.

As we do, we gain trust.

In the *Speed of Trust*, author Stephen M.R. Covey describes integrity, intent, capabilities, and results as the four cores of credibility (or trust).

Our response time in communication is an immediate (or not-so-immediate result).

The timeframes in which we respond to all forms of communication give the people with whom we work an immediate "result" on which to judge us. This will either build or decay trust.

"Wow! I didn't expect a response so quickly. Thank you." versus "Did you see may email? I have sent it a few times."

These are vastly different statements.

MEDIUM

Which medium of communication do you prefer?

Face-to-Face Meeting

Phone call

Virtual Meeting

Email

Text Message

Internal Messaging System

Social Media

The answer for most readers is immediately, "It depends."

This is absolutely correct. The level at which we need discussion and the subject matter are just two of the litany of variables needed to answer the question.

But, in general, which do you prefer?

We all have a preference.

I hate phone calls.

I seriously hate them, and I am not sure why.

I love face-to-face. Always.

I also love a text message. Don't email me, though, please.

If you want a response, just text.

A cross-generational leader will balance both ends of this spectrum in communication with our team. We should work to understand individual tendencies, as well as explain the need for certain types of communication regardless of anyone's preference.

How we achieve this balance:

1. Ask
2. Accommodate
3. Avoid

Ask your team. Don't assume. Ask.

Speak openly with your team about their preferred methods for different types of messages. Ask if they need a meeting or if emails are helpful.

Many, if not most, communication pitfalls can be avoided if we will simply ask.

Accommodate every which way you can.

We can often fall prey to the way something "should" be.

We "should" have a meeting about that.

That "should" be an email, not an instant message.

All bets are off.

How do you best communicate, and how do you want to communicate? Cross generations desire information formatted differently. Some will prefer face-to-face interaction, while for some, an email will do. Voicemails, texts, memorandums, posts on an interoffice board, Facebook, or Twitter can all be valid mediums, but not all will be effective cross-generationally. Know your audience and choose the medium that works the best for them. Chances are you will use multiple forms of communication per message. There are so many methods of communication available…choose what works best for your team as a whole and individually.

Avoid personal preference. We should be quick to serve and slow to judge. If a team member needs a little more face time, try to give it to them. If you prefer a conference call, but everyone wants an email, make the team happy.

You can't always accommodate but you should never choose something because you want it.

MESSAGE

What am I saying?

Is the medium in which I am sharing my message effective?

What medium fits best?

What weight does the medium give the message?

Inevitably, your message is the essential element of your communication. It is the heartbeat of your company. It informs your branding, your marketing, your buying decisions, and your partnerships. If your message — what you have to say to the world through your products, services, or ideas — do not line up, you will struggle to succeed. We think holistically about messaging when we think of a company, but it fits your individual leadership also.

What is your message?

What is your leadership brand?

What do you want it to be?

The words you choose are important.

If something is important to me, I will work to understand it. This is nowhere more evident than language.

I have had the absolute honor of speaking multiple times in multiple countries. When traveling abroad, people respond when you earnestly try to learn their language. Could you look like a fool? Maybe.

Will you mess up? Sometimes. But words, names, and meanings are important to people. We should take the same attitude when working with folks who are younger or older than us.

Speed, medium, and message indicate to your team members their importance to you. When people feel valued, heard, and honored in this way, the efforts they put into their work increases. Community grows, and productivity, by extension, increases.

Mindful communication is imperative for healthy cross-generational leadership.

Inherently we know this, but since we still struggle with communication, it begs the question, what are we missing? I believe the breakdown happens sooner than we think. When we get a new team member, or we are building a team, one of the first questions we should ask is this: How do you prefer to communicate?

When we know how people like to communicate, we can identify potential communication pitfalls between ourselves and the multigenerational teams we lead. Remember, we do not have a generational problem; we have a leadership problem, and the simple question, "How do you prefer to communicate?" goes a long way to closing this gap.

CHAPTER 7: WHAT WE ALL WANT

"Leadership is the ability to guide others without force into a direction or decision that leaves them still feeling empowered and accomplished."

- Lisa Cash Hanson

What connects us is infinitely stronger than what divides us.

Across millennia, humans have searched for purpose.

It fills our art in all forms.

Music, movies, poetry and books across time examine purpose, love, and the meaning of life.

People from all generations wrestle with the largest of questions.

Where did this begin? Where does it end? Is this it?

As cross-generational leaders this gives us opportunity.

We have the opportunity to help people find meaning in the everyday.

All people.

All generations.

Every generation wrestles with the largest questions of our existence and the relevance of our lives.

What makes us the same is more powerful than what makes us different.

We are all searching for something.

Leaders can help us find it.

While all our journeys are unique, there are some broad qualities that we all need in some form or fashion.

Tony Robbins first introduced six human needs at a TED conference with a talk entitled: "Why We Do the Things We Do." With an audience that included politicians, billionaires, and world leaders, Robbins categorized all of humanity collectively with the following six basic human needs.

1. **Certainty:** assurance you can avoid pain and gain pleasure
2. **Uncertainty/Variety:** the need for the unknown, change, new stimuli
3. **Significance:** feeling unique, important, special, or needed
4. **Connection/Love:** a strong feeling of closeness or union with someone or something

5. **Growth:** an expansion of capacity, capability, or understanding
6. **Contribution:** a sense of service and focus on helping, giving to and supporting others

"Everybody has goals and desires that are different, but we have the same needs."

- Tony Robbins

Robbins further explains that these core needs drive every decision we make.

All dysfunctional behaviors arise from the inability to consistently meet these core needs. But people's needs aren't just behind the bad decisions we make — they are also behind all of the great things humans accomplish. Understanding your own needs and psychology can not only help you avoid toxic behaviors and habits but can also help you achieve your goals.[25]

One habit many mindful leaders have adopted is to consider these six basic needs when shaping healthy work environments for multiple generations. Good leadership can recognize these needs as both the root of problematic behavior and the fuel for phenomenal contribution.

We can use these as a compass when developing policies, events, performance reviews, or reward programs. We can ask ourselves which of these

[25] https://www.tonyrobbins.com/mind-meaning/do-you-need-to-feel-significant/

needs isn't being met when we see stress, conflict, or chaos.

We all interpret these needs differently. Our childhood, our personal beliefs, and our current situations all influence *how* we need these essentials met.

The first four needs listed shape our personality, while the last two shape our spiritual needs.

Everyone ranks these human needs differently and each can be met in a variety of ways.

These can all be met to some degree in the workplace.

Namely, certainty and significance.

CERTAINTY AND SIGNIFICANCE

Certainty is the need to feel safe and secure about the future.

The terms certainty, safety, and security are interchangeable for our purposes.

As humans, we all need safety.

The need for safety was acknowledged as a basic human need by Abraham Maslow in his Hierarchy of Needs. Safety needs represent the second tier in Maslow's hierarchy and these needs include the security of body, of employment, of resources, of morality, of family, and of health.[26]

Maslow's Hierarchy of Needs are physiological, safety, love, esteem, and self-actualization. He theorized that as we achieve those needs motivation increases, and as those needs are unmet, we lose motivation. In the workplace, we can see increased performance and output as we help our teams fulfill their needs.

Physiological needs are the biological requirements for human survival. They include the classic food, water, and shelter trio.

If these needs are not satisfied, the human body cannot function optimally. Maslow considered physiological needs the most important, as all the other needs become secondary until these needs are met.

Once an individual's physiological needs are satisfied, the needs for security and safety become salient. People want to experience order, predictability, and control in their lives. These needs can be fulfilled by the family and society.

For example, emotional security, financial security, and law all contribute to our second level of needs being met.

---

[26] https://www.interaction-design.org/literature/article/safety-maslow-s-hierarchy-of-needs

Job security helps achieve the first and second levels of human need.

Job security, however, has changed over the last half century.

We understand that recession, corruption, or market erosion can occur at any moment.

Most of us understand that we could lose our jobs at any moment.

There are worldwide systems out of our control that could hit our industry...and hit it hard. Acts of God, war, and other catastrophic incidents are beyond control.

Additionally, we don't have the same level of institutional trust that we had years ago.

According to the Edelman Trust Barometer, trust in governments, media, and economies is lower than ever. The Covid-19 pandemic, with more than 1.9 million lives lost and joblessness equivalent to the Great Depression, has accelerated the erosion of trust around the world. This is evident in the significant drop in trust in the two largest economies: the U.S. and China. The U.S. (40 percent) and Chinese (30 percent) governments are deeply distrusted by respondents from the 26 other markets surveyed. And most notable is the drop in trust among their own citizens, with the U.S., already in the bottom quartile for trust, experiencing an additional 5-point drop since its presidential election in November 2020 and China seeing an 18-point drop since May 2020.[27]

In a world full of uncertainty, how can we provide certainty as a leader?

If people don't trust institutions, how do we build trust?

People mistrust institutions, but they still trust people.

They can trust you.

HABITS OF INCLUSION

As a leader, most of us cannot guarantee someone job security.

Not only are we vulnerable to all the above scenarios, but internally we may not have the final word.

Budget cuts, layoff, and positional realignment may very well be out of our hands.

Our teams know this. They understand that job security is a myth. They understand that their boss has a boss. You, as a supervisor, may not be able to protect them no matter what.

But you can try.

You can always try.

Does your team trust that you have their back?

---

[27] https://www.edelman.com/trust/2021-trust-barometer

Do they know that you are always advocating for them?

They may not trust the organization, but they trust you.

They trust you to not to protect them from bad news, but to share it with them.

This is inclusion.

Good leaders are inclusive leaders.

While the topic of diversity and inclusion is too deep and broad for this conversation, we can start.

If we are going to truly have greater equity and inclusion initiatives, it will start with personal beliefs and daily habits. We must show people certainty and security by consistently demonstrating a value of their best interests. We must include people in our decision-making processes, our organizational circumstances, and our personal convictions. This isn't achieved in a one-time dramatic demonstration. It occurs when we invite, applaud, share, and help. These four verbs instill security in our team over time.

INVITE

An invitation may be the most powerful act we possess as humans. We have the power to invite people into our lives, into our inner circle, or into our worldview. These larger ideals are accomplished gradually as we invite people to lunch, invite them to our table, or invite them into our space.

APPLAUD

Alan McGinnis in his book *Bringing Out the Best in People* shares the idea of a bandwagon. "If anyone is going close to where you are going, jump on their bandwagon."

This is applause. We should always actively look for ways to brag on our team and our peers. If you want people to trust you more, see the best in them. Look for the good.

Praise people openly, often, and loudly.

Criticize people privately, rarely, and quietly.

SHARE

As leaders, we are the keepers of information. Share this information with people. It starts with sharing positivity and praise…that's applause. It continues with sharing your honest feedback, genuine concern, and truthful circumstances.

Miguel Ruiz in *The Four Agreements* says, "If others tell us something we make assumptions, and if they don't tell us something we make assumptions to fulfill our need to know and to replace the need to communicate. Even if we hear something and we don't understand, we make assumptions about what it means and then believe the assumptions. We make all sorts of assumptions because we don't have the courage to ask questions."[28]

Share frequently with people to counter assumptions.

Share your questions to understand clearly.

HELP

Earlier in this book, we shared the John Adams' letter:

I must study Politicks and War so that my sons may have liberty to study Painting and Poetry Mathematicks and Philosophy. My sons ought to study Mathematics and Philosophy, Geography, natural History, Navel Architecture, navigation, Commerce and Agriculture, in order to give their children a right to study Painting, Poetry, Musick, Architecture, Statuary, Tapestry, and Porcelaine. [sic]

This may strike a chord with us, especially those of us who are parents.

We may empathize completely when we think of our children, or nephews, or cousins, or people we know and love.

But what about the people in your office?

---

[28] *The Four Agreements: A Practical Guide to Personal Freedom (A Toltec Wisdom Book)* by Don Miguel Ruiz

Do you feel the same compulsion to create a better world for them?

We can.

Each of us can help others. Rather than a "me first" mentality, we can help others.

"I figured it out, so can you."

"No one showed me."

"I'm not paid enough to do both our jobs."

This exclusive language is selfish and shortsighted.

Helping others may be sacrificial in the moment, but it is building your reputation in the long run.

People need security.

These four habits of inclusion can help them have it.

SIGNIFICANCE

People want to feel significant.

People want to feel valued at work.

The Employee Experience Imperative study finds employees who feel "heard and valued" have better morale and performance.

55% of respondents didn't feel their opinions mattered to their bosses.

Half of the employees polled weren't sure that their employers would offer any support during major life events like parental or medical leave.

Just 37% believed their employers' process-automation efforts were done to improve the worker experience.[29]

Measurable business benefits were uncovered by "The Heard and the Heard-Nots", a global study of over 4,000 employees, conducted by The Workforce Institute at UKG and Workplace Intelligence.

- Highly engaged employees are three times more likely to say they feel heard at their workplace (92%) than highly disengaged employees (just 30%).
- 74% of employees report they are more effective at their job when they feel heard.
- 88% of employees whose companies financially outperform others in their industry feel heard compared to 62% of employees at financially underperforming companies.

Yet, despite the tangible benefits to financial performance, productivity, and engagement, a high majority of employees (86%) feel that people at their workplace are not heard fairly or equally.

---

[29] https://www.businessnewsdaily.com/15272-employee-experience engagement.html

Essential workers, younger workers, and parents are the three groups tagged as most underrepresented.[30]

This a more than just a generational issue.

"There are four generations in today's workforce: baby boomers, Gen X, millennials and Gen Z. Typically, researchers can find differences between the groups, but these researchers said they found that the need for a good employee experience transcends age."[31]

All this information points toward one need: significance.

Engaged employees feel significant at their workplace.

They feel valued.

They feel heard.

Are you listening to them?

Caroline Ceniza-Levine, senior contributor for Forbes, says it this way, "If you care about company culture, these findings give even more reasons to aim for inclusive teams. You can help employees feel heard in everyday actions. No need to wait for an official employee engagement survey or campaign organized by HR. In the course of your

---

[30] https://www.ukg.com/about-us/newsroom/silenced-workforce-four-in-five-employees-feel-colleagues-arent-heard-equally-says-research-workforce-institute-ukg
[31] https://www.businessnewsdaily.com/15272-employee-experience engagement.html

day-to-day work, there is ample opportunity to let people feel heard."[32]

THE PEOPLE HAVE SPOKEN

How do we take this information and put it into practical use?

The Good Leader Podcast recently held a four-week campaign on cross-generational leadership.[33] They interviewed leaders in all four working generations and asked what they were looking for in a leader. While the answers varied, all participants had three shared traits.

That's right!

Without prompting, and without multiple choice, every single generation said the same three answers. Baby Boomers, Gen X, Millennial, and Gen Z are all looking for these traits in a leader.

1. Be a learner.
2. Listen.
3. Give people an opportunity to succeed.

That's it.

---

[32]

https://www.forbes.com/sites/carolinecenizalevine/2021/06/23/new-survey-shows-the-business-benefit-of-feeling-heard--5-ways-to-build-inclusive-teams/?sh=4642e2cc5f0c

[33] Ok, ok…it is our podcast. But it's pretty decent. You should check it out. Download "The Good Leader Podcast" from your local podcast dealer.

No need for exposition or elaboration.

If you want to hear more from these responses, check out the podcast.

Better yet, listen to them as a team.

PART 3

BEST PRACTICES OF CROSS-
GENERATIONAL ORGANIZATIONS.

CHAPTER 8: RETENTION

"Take this job and shove it, I ain't working here no more."

- Johnny Paycheck

There is a war on talent.

If you want to win you have to change your perspectives.

Many of them.

In a war, you have an enemy. Who is your enemy in the war on talent?

The talent? Doubtful.

Your industry competition? Maybe.

The real enemy? You.

Me, myself, and I are the real enemy.

If you change your perspective, you might see something for the first time.

I am convinced that good people are going to continue to do good work.

The question is, for whom?

If we are going to be outstanding cross-generational leaders, we must change several of our views.

We must change the way we view time.

We must change the way we view loyalty.

We must change the way we view retention.

Redefine time.

Redefine loyalty.

Refine retention.

That's cross-generational leadership.

THE GREAT RESIGNATION

The "war for talent" is a term coined by Steven Hankin of McKinsey & Company in 1997, and a book by the same name in 2001.[34] The war for talent refers to an increasingly competitive landscape for recruiting and retaining talented employees.

According to an article by Guild Education, "The demographic and societal forces that kicked off the war for talent have only become more intense. Baby boomers are retiring earlier than expected and in increasing numbers. In addition, 1 in 4 employees across generations are planning to change jobs as the pandemic subsides. With uncertainty around

---

[34] Ed Michaels, Helen Handfield-Jones, and Beth Axelrod, Harvard Business Press, 2001 ISBN 978-1-57851-459-5.

childcare access and school closures, nearly 3 million women have left the labor force — and it remains to be seen how those numbers will bounce back. College enrollment is also on the decline, so skilled talent is not being as readily replenished.

These trends have led to the lowest labor force participation rate since the 70s. And with a slowing population growth rate, there are simply not enough workers to fill open roles.

"The original war for talent was focused on executives and leadership skills (and that focus is still relevant), but today, the breadth of missing skills is greater.

Automation and digital transformation have increased competition for jobs: 69% of companies reported talent shortages last year, the highest number in a decade. Manufacturing plants are having trouble hiring workers, logistics companies need more truck drivers, and restaurants are struggling to attract enough talent to get by, let alone grow. Many companies are increasing wages and offering hiring bonuses in response, but often still struggle to retain or effectively develop that talent. A higher wage will fill some roles today, but it won't build the skills your company needs for the future or create the engagement that will lead to long-term retention.

"In 2016, Millennials became the largest generation in the U.S. labor force. They have higher rates of job mobility, more demands for flexibility, but most importantly, they care about mission and corporate social responsibility. Studies have found that Millennials will make sacrifices for the issues they care about, whether by paying a premium (70%), sharing products (66%), or even taking a lower salary to work for a more responsible company.

"Both Millennials and Gen Z have grown up in the midst of a growing climate emergency, widespread racial injustice, and expanding economic inequality. They want change, and they want it from their employers. In May 2021, the Edelman Trust Barometer revealed that employees expect employers to take action on social problems including climate change (81%), automation (79%), and racism (79%)."[35]

The number of American workers quitting their jobs hit record highs in November 2021, with 4.5 million people walking off the job, according to the latest Bureau of Labor Statistics report.

"While job openings decreased in November, hires held steady as quits continued to rise. Hiring remains higher than quits, suggesting that some who quit may be finding better opportunities within the sector," wrote Elise Gould, a senior economist with the progressive Economic Policy Institute. In fact, while the overall quit rate across all industries is high, it's important to note that hiring is even higher. "Hires are on an upswing as quits continue

---

[35] https://blog.guildeducation.com/the-war-for-talent-is-the-new-normal/

to rise. Workers appear confident to quit their jobs in search of better ones," Gould noted.[36]

The war on talent rages.

The great resignation is real.

Employees have the upper hand.

Prudential Vice Chair Rob Falzon says, "If there's one thing that keeps me up at night, it's the talent flight risk."

They are definitely flying, Rob…*what do we do?*

TIME AND THE GIG ECONOMY

Oxford languages defines the "gig economy" as a labor market characterized by the prevalence of short-term contracts or freelance work as opposed to permanent jobs.

Gig's origin is uncertain. The earliest usage of the word *gig* in the sense of "any, usual temporary, paid job" is from a 1952 piece by Jack Kerouac about his gig as a part-time brakeman for the Southern Pacific railroad.[37]

---

[36] https://fortune.com/2022/01/04/great-resignation-record-quit-rate-4-5-million/
[37] Geoffrey Nunberg (January 11, 2016). "Goodbye Jobs, Hello 'Gigs': How One Word Sums Up A New Economic Reality." *Fresh Air*. NPR. Retrieved January 24, 2020.

36% of U.S. workers join in the gig economy through either their primary or secondary jobs.[38]

A study by the McKinsey Global Institute concluded that, across America and England, there were a total of 162 million people that were involved in some type of independent work.[39]

The gig economy is more than a side hustle or temporary position.

It is an atmosphere that focuses on skillset and opportunity more than a degree or previous experience.

It creates opportunities focused on projects and outcomes rather than hours and formalities.

The gig economy changes the way work gets done.

We have changed the way work gets done.

Rather than getting dressed in business attire, commuting an hour into the office, and working a full eight-hour day, many employees can get in their favorite joggers, slip on some comfortable shoes, and sit at their kitchen table to do the work they have tasked for the day.

According to the Market Inspector, a blog based in the United Kingdom, Millennials enjoy workplace

---

[38] Pendell, Ryan; McFeely, Shane (August 16, 2018). "What Workplace Leaders Can Learn From the Real Gig Economy." *Gallup*.
[39] "Independent work: Choice, necessity, and the gig economy." *McKinsey & Company*

flexibility. They seek a work-life balance and prefer to look at work as something to do to earn money rather than a place to go or a career path.[40]

We must change our perception of time.

Is a workday still 9-5? Is a work week 40 hours?

Gigs are gigs because they are thought to be short.

Careers are careers because they are thought to be long.

What if every job, every career, every day was a gig?

We must change the way we think about time.

LOYALTY AND RAVING FANS

Summer of 2016 crushed my soul.

Specifically, July 4, Independence Day, crushed my soul.

The free agency of Kevin Durant crushed my soul.

For basketball fans, you know who Kevin Durant is.

For non-basketball fans, here is all you need to know.

He is good at basketball.

Like, *really good.*

---

[40] https://www.market-inspector.co.uk/blog/2017/03/the-work-habits-of-millennials

Like, hall of fame, once in a lifetime, top 10 player of all time good.

And he played for my beloved Oklahoma City Thunder.

The Oklahoma City Thunder are a small market NBA team in an all-out brawl for talent. Kevin Durant was the centerpiece of our team, the cornerstone of our franchise, and the key to our future.

With our beautiful team he won an MVP, scoring titles, and almost a championship.

Then 2016 free agency arrived.

His contract was up for renewal, and he could choose anywhere to play.

He didn't choose us. He chose the Golden State Devils...I mean...Warriors...

The OKC Thunder faithful were crushed. We were angry.

"How could they leave us?"

"We have a great organization."

"We did everything we could for them."

Maybe these statements sound familiar in your organization with your retention efforts. We live in a player-controlled era in sports. Likewise, workers want to determine their work future.

As a fan of the Oklahoma City Thunder, Durant's free agency was either disappointing, heart-breaking, or infuriating.

But, as a fan of Kevin Durant, his move to Golden State was exciting, amazing, and opportunistic!

Are you a bigger fan of your people or the company name?

Jerry Seinfeld famously joked that sports fans were really fans of laundry.

"It's different guys every year," Jerry Seinfeld observed. "You're rooting for clothes, when you get right down to it. We're screaming about laundry."

We, too, can fall into the same trap.

We cheer for the team (the company name), not the players.

The real players.

The people. They are our team.

We must be raving fans of our people.

They, in turn, will be raving fans of us.

We work so hard on retention efforts, but we live in a free agency era.

Opportunities abound and people will leave.

All people. Every single person.

There isn't a single person connected to your organization that won't leave given the right circumstances.

Not one. You would leave. I would leave.

Kevin Durant would leave.

Even the founder, the owner, the main man or woman would leave.

Given the right circumstances, we all may leave.

If someone offers us an amazing salary, an amazing opportunity, or an amazing location, of course we are going to go.

That's not even considering personal life values or situations.

That's ok.

That isn't disloyal. That's normal.

Kevin Durant took a new job at an awesome company with amazing teammates.

It wasn't personal to the fans.

Do we like it? No.

Can I understand it? Yes.

We must change the way we define loyalty. I can be a raving fan of the company *and* the players. I can be happy when our current team does well and when my former teammates do well elsewhere.

Wait…why are they my *former* teammates?

Time has changed, remember? Someone can be on my proverbial team forever.

It is all about your perception.

They may not be in the same office now, but are they still a resource?

Will you never, ever, ever work with them or for them again?

Never is a long time.

We must change the way we think about time.

We must change the way we think about loyalty.

We must change the way we think about retention.

RETENTION AND THE NEW REPLACEMENT

Employee retention is defined as an organization's ability to prevent employee turnover.

Retention/turnover was the top workforce management challenge cited by 47% of HR professionals in the SHRM/Globoforce survey, "Using Recognition and Other Workplace Efforts to Engage Employees."[41]

The truth is, you can do everything right in your role as a leader and still lose good people. Instead of looking at it as only negative, we can change our thinking.

We have to or we will drive ourselves crazy.

---

[41] https://www.shrm.org/hr-today/trends-and-forecasting/research-and-surveys/pages/employee-recognition-2018.aspx

We should focus on retention, but we should think more broadly.

By all means, work to keep good people on your team.

But balance that with a healthy understanding that they may leave.

They probably will.

In addition to your retention rate, consider your quality replacement rate.

Your Quality Retention Rate (QRR) is the time it takes to match productivity when someone leaves. If someone leaves in your company, would it be a disaster?

For some people yes, others no.

Think of a highly productive member of your team. If they left abruptly tomorrow, how long would it take to replace them and replicate their output? Would the process and training take one year, one month, or one week?

That is your Quality Replacement Rate.

The goal can still be to increase your retention rate.

But also work to decrease your quality replacement rate.

A solid Quality Replacement Rate is achieved through a combination of three major factors: succession planning, substitution recruitment, and transition lead time.

SUCCESSION PLANNING

More than previous generations, upcoming generations prefer to craft a job or make it their own. Though they have a reputation for being lazy, Millennials are, in fact, workaholics. From Canada to Japan, Mexico to the Netherlands, and the USA to Singapore, Millennials work anywhere between 43 to 52 hours a week on average. Their ambition is less about corporate movement and more about doing good work.

Millennials are a mobile generation. USA Today reports Millennials are twice as likely to resign one position for a more lucrative or interesting one than people in more established generations. One reason Millennials feel a need for lateral moves between companies is the opportunity they see for promotion.[42]

Does your workforce see opportunity for career promotion and personal growth in your organization?

This begins with training.

Specifically, the way we approach training and adult learning.

---

[42]

https://www.usatoday.com/story/money/careers/employment-trends/2018/06/11/why-millennials-resign-more-than-older-workers/35921637/

Succession planning is the process of identifying the critical positions within your organization and developing action plans for individuals to assume those positions.

The best succession planning isn't just identifying who may leave or retire soon and who will take their job.

Many succession plans are simply glorified talent labeling:

"We used nine box one time and found out who has a lot of potential."

Eighty percent of CEOS now believe the need for new skills is their biggest business challenge.

For employees, research now shows that opportunities for development have become the second most important factor in workplace happiness (after the nature of the work itself).[43]

If we are going to create a successful succession plan, we must have a culture of learning. Adult learning.

Specifically, we should understand andragogy versus pedagogy.

Andragogy is a combination from two words, "andre" (from the Greek word man) and "gogy" (from the Greek for leader). Pedagogy is a similar

---

[43] Harvard Business Review: Make Learning a Part of Everyday Work

amalgamation but with "pedi" for child.[44] As a teacher, speaker, and leader I value any methodology which helps students learn.

Children learn out of a natural curiosity. They observe the world and learn precept by precept. Curriculum-based learning is the proven method to educate kids. As they master one principle, they can move on to learn more complex ones. Adult learners possess different motivations and therefore learn differently.

There are seven tenants of adult learning.[45]

1. Adults cannot be forced to learn.
2. Adults will only learn what they feel they must (relevance rules).
3. Adults learn by experience.
4. Adults learn to solve problems.
5. An adult's past affects their learning
6. Adults learn informally.
7. Adults want information, not guidance as kids do.

The idea that adults learn differently than children was first introduced by German educator Alexander Kaap, but advanced by American educator Malcolm Knowles.

---

[44] (https://www.lexico.com/definition/andragogy)
[45] https://challenges.openideo.com/challenge/refugee-education/research/the-seven-principles-of-adult-learning)

From the 1950s to the 1990s, Knowles advanced the precepts listed above and changed the way we educate adults.[46]

Adults learn out of necessity. If they do not find a new idea or technology applicable, then they will be reluctant, or even adverse, to learning it. In fact, established generations are more likely to judge a new methodology, idea, or technology than learn and implement it into their life.

Knowing this, how can we create learning systems that attract talent and value individuals as unique learners?

We can now share our "why" with the team and align with the "why" that motivates each person individually.

SUBSTITUTION RECRUITMENT

Sometimes the best succession planning isn't with your current people.

Sometimes the best successor is recruited by your current team.

Substitution recruitment is your team helping you build your team.

When they are on their way out, do they help someone find their way in?

---

[46] https://www.instructionaldesign.org/theories/andragogy/

In the book *Raving Fans*, Ken Blanchard and Sheldon Howes teach us to "create a vision of perfection centered around your customer."

This creates raving fans.

Your team is your top customer. Treat them in such a way that they want to help you.

When they leave, they still want you to succeed.

They can feel that they are still on the team.

TRANSITION LEAD TIME

Time has changed.

It may be customary to give two weeks' notice, but that is completely arbitrary.

Tradition without meaning is worthless.

Generally speaking, the longer we have to process someone's departure, the more equipped we will be. We may be able to hire their substitute before they depart.

This decreases your Quality Replacement Rate.

For healthier transition lead times, organizations must work through a few areas.

First, we must negate fear.

Many people assume their job will be in jeopardy if they express an intent to leave.

If this is the case, stop here.

Change your company culture *immediately*.

You have to be willing to openly accept both a person's arrival and departure well.

Second, honor those that leave.

Good riddance should never be the mantra.

When someone leaves, this is often the green light to share all your grievances with the team. This should never be the case, especially from managerial staff.

Celebrate people as they leave.

Work to genuinely see their perspective and honor them.

Third, don't take it personally.

It has been said many times that "people don't leave bad jobs, they leave bad bosses."

This isn't completely true.

Do people leave bad bosses? Sure. Sometimes.

Do people stay because of good bosses? Sure. Sometimes.

But sometimes, many times, people leave *situations*.

As a leader, we cannot take it personally.

RETENTION IS TOUGH.

Those who win are going to change the way they view retention.

It isn't a war for talent, as much as a long game with lots of moving players.

Play the game.

Don't fight a war with no real enemy.

Create raving fans from your employees.

You can do all the right things in your company — create culture, pay well, train well, and promote well — and still lose talent. Do not think this is a generational issue.

It is merely the new nature of the business.

Control is a misconception, retention is elusive, but fandom is a commodity we can earn if we understand how it works. To create raving fans, we have to be fans. To understand the complexity of fandom, we must understand the complexity of our team's individual agendas.

Redefine time.

Redefine loyalty.

Refine retention.

That's cross-generational leadership.

CHAPTER 9: CULTURE AND CORE VALUES

"It's not hard to make decisions when you know what your core values are."

- Roy Disney

WHO TEACHES THE ROBOTS RIGHT FROM WRONG?

Our company cultures must be built on core values.

It will become even more important in the future.

Tim Elmore, author of *Marching Off the Map*, shares four ages of history so far, and the key driver for each.[47]

In the agricultural age, the key driver was our muscles.

In the industrial age, the key driver was our minds.

---

[47] *Marching Off the Map: Inspire Students to Navigate a Brand New World* by Tim Elmore, January 1, 2017

In the information age, the key driver has been our minds.

In the automation age, the key driver will be our morals.

Morals can be tricky.

We haven't shared the same values for a while now.

As society evolves, our values, our morals, have become more diversified.

As new generations enter the workforce, multigenerational values become more divided. When one generation sees another generation doing something they deem as ridiculous, it's because the values they hold as important are not shared with the other generation.

We can no longer assume people share the same value system.

Traits, characteristics, and ideals that were obvious just two generations ago are now debatable. Even a list of American ideals from a government website have traits like independence, consumerism, and individualism, which almost encourage differing opinions amongst team members.

With such differing opinions of what we should or should not do in any given situation, it is more stretching than ever for us to create unity.

We will discuss three practices of good cross-generational leaders to create more unity in any organization.

- Clarify and utilize your core values as an organization.
- Understand the key identifiers of company culture
- Move from practices of assimilation to acculturation.

CORE VALUES

We don't want blind conformity from our teams.

We want people to think for themselves.

We want them to contribute new ideas and feel the liberty to share them.

These ideas and contributions, however, must align with a larger whole. The collective ideals of our organization are, in fact, what our organization is.

Core values define companies.

Not the buildings, or the logo, or even the products.

All of those can change rapidly.

What should not change rapidly are core values.

When leaders fully adopt values-based leadership, they position themselves to serve their people better. People from different generations can bring their generational ideals with them to work, but our shared values guide us while we are here.

Most people, most organizations, don't use core values properly.

Core values should be your guidepost. Your beacon. Your lighthouse.

They should be discussed frequently and understood deeply.

They should be used in the hiring process and in performance reviews.

They should be considered in decision-making and project adoption.

Instead, they are often a stale mission statement on the wall or some combination of words that are flat or meaningless.

How many of your team can name your company's core values?

How many of them work to fulfill them daily?

How many of them consciously consider them when making decisions?

How often do you or other leaders mention your core values?

We must do a better job of choosing and implementing our values throughout our entire operation. This may be the single greatest task of a leader.

How do we instill belief in these shared values and create buy-in from our people?

These values will then guide each team member when operating within their jobs and tasks. These values become the common thread that informs each person's decisions, priorities, and choices in the day-to-day operations of your business. Without these, we allow for more broad interpretation of the right thing do in any given situation.

Roy Disney said, "It's not hard to make decisions when you know what your core values are."

We want to build decision makers.

Outstanding cross-generational leadership uses shared values to bring people from all generations together in a common cause.

COMPANY CULTURE

Describe your company culture.

When asked to do this, people often give broad adjectives that are largely up for interpretation.

Our company culture is good.

We are like a family.

Our culture is busy.

We don't do a very good job of describing our company culture because we don't understand culture that well.

It is a leader's job to create culture.

Culture exists to achieve desired results.

What are your desired results?

If you answer anything besides your stated core values, then your core values are incorrect.

If your gut response to "What are your desired results?" is "sales", then sales are your core value.

If your response was satisfied customers, then satisfied customers are your desired results.

Sales, profit, revenue, and customers should all be benefits of your core values.

In other words, if you choose your core values purposefully and live them out, these benefits will follow.

Your core values should drive your culture and your culture will see those benefits.

How do we create a culture that is both driven by and drives core values?

There are four major identifiers of culture: language, art, food, and values.

You should be intentional with these four areas to drive your core values.

There is no specific right or wrong with any of these.

They simply reflect or reveal your culture.

What language do you use, promote, and adopt in your workplace?

Is it positive?

Is it inclusive?

Is it derogatory?

What art do people experience in your work environments?

Art isn't just painting, sculpting, or drawing.

Art is the expression of human creative skill and imagination.

In the workplace, art is all our combined sensory experiences.

What people wear. What is on the wall. What your emails look like.

All art.

Your environment tells us a lot about your culture.

What does your interaction with food reveal about your culture?

Food is important to humans.

Various foods are connected to important life events or holidays.

What is on your Thanksgiving table, Christmas dinner, or birthday party menu?

How do you use food to build culture?

What do you have to do to earn a cake or free meal?

Who eats with whom?

Where do you take your lunch?

How are your core values demonstrated?

Yes, they are on the wall.

Yes, they are in the handbook.

But your values should be the bedrock of your culture. You should make them matter. You should display them uniquely. You should discuss them frequently.

How do you know if you are using these four identifiers well?

Notice these four identifiers are without age restriction.

Forward thinking cross-generational leaders realize that while generations may have different perceptions, we can come together in our company culture.

AGEISM, ASSIMILATION, AND ACCULTURATION

There are two key questions that you can ask as an organization to measure your culture:

What do you celebrate?

What would an outsider notice?

We often believe we have a strong culture when we do not. Our experience may be completely different than most of our team. These two questions help break our potential tunnel vision and think of culture in a new way.

Culture done well can create community.

The word community comes from the word "communis", meaning "common, public, shared by all or many." The English term "communication" evolved from two Latin words, "communis" and "communicare." While communis is a noun, the word communicare is a verb which means, "make something common."

In the past, community meant our neighbors —the general area we live, work, and play in — but today, thanks to the interconnectedness of the world at large through social media and the internet in general, our sense of community looks different.

We, therefore, have to be more intentional about creating community at work.

In truth, people don't need it anymore.

If we want to create community, it has to be based on our agreed shared values.

Those must be communicated frequently to "make these common."

Strong communities are the only answer against discrimination.

All kinds of discrimination. Racism. Sexism. Ageism.

Thankfully, many of us have become more aware of our own biases and how we've stereotyped others in the past. When launching Disney+, the Walt Disney Company put disclaimers on many of their older movies because cultural sensitivity is higher now than it was in past years.

This is important work, and we still have much work to do on all fronts.

Ageism may be the least discussed.

Do a quick Google search for the definition of discrimination, and you will find it means a few things. I want to focus on two aspects of the word. First, discriminate means *"to differentiate between or to identify the quality of one element from another."* As leaders, we see different characteristics, qualities, capabilities, and callings in our people. Rightly discriminating is one of the abilities that make us good leaders. When we cross over into the second definition of discrimination, *"the unjust or prejudicial treatment of different categories of people or things, especially on the grounds of race, age, or sex"*, we lose our footing.

Ageism is not new, but countries are reporting an increase in age bias, particularly against women. Sixty-one percent of US workers at or over the age of 45 reported witnessing or experiencing ageism in the workplace. Among European companies, ageism is the most common type of discrimination. More than 44% of the respondents interviewed reported concern over discrimination. In the 27 years between 1990 and 2017, the Equal Employment Opportunity Commission reported a 15% increase in the number of Age Discrimination complaints filed by women at or over the age of forty. In the same period, charges by men in the same age range decreased by 18%.[48]

This statistic points to the trend of gendered ageism, which is ageism targeted at one gender over the other. As the fastest-growing population, women aged 55 and over will constitute more than one-third of new hires joining the workforce. The misconception that age affects ability leads companies to create workplaces that are quick to welcome the young and even quicker to dismiss older people.

For a while, the world, in order to eliminate discrimination, advocated for assimilation. Assimilation asks people to shed their cultural backgrounds to create uniformity. Instead, as leaders, we should shift our paradigm to acculturation.[49]

(Authors note: I was introduced to acculturation by the work of Juana Bordas, and the book *Salsa, Soul, and Spirit: Leadership for a Multicultural Age*. It is a fantastic read. Now, on with the show.)

Acculturation allows employees to see other cultures — they adapt, receive, and build skills to interact with them — while keeping their own culture.

---

[48] Sophia Ahn abd Anekua Costigan, Trend Brief: Gendered Ageism (Catalyst, 2019)
[49] *Salsa, Soul and Spirit: Leadership for a Multicultural Age* by Juana Bordas (2012)

How far would this one practice take us?

It is more honoring and respectful than not "seeing color" or not "noticing age." The selective blindness of assimilation removes a large part of someone's humanity and story. Acculturation is a better practice than assimilation. Acculturation allows people to work in a broader spectrum than the homogeny of assimilation.

When we focus on core values as a company, we create a new culture together.

We are all a part of many cultures. We bring them to the workplace as we create community together.

All "isms" (ageism, racism, sexism, etc.) only work because they divide people into categories which are easily labeled by language. Them, They, and Those People — you've heard these things before. You may have said one or more of these phrases yourself. Perhaps it was in the context of political views, or you were despairing over the bosses' lack of leadership, or maybe you were angry about people who own the gas station down your street. The language of them/they are a crucial indicator of culture, and it reveals our own bias and hidden assumptions.

Instead of them and they, we should strive to use inclusive language — especially in the workplace. Inclusive language is an all-in venture. Saying "we" and "us" challenges us to take responsibility for the health, wellness, productivity, success, and failures of our team. Inclusive language builds relationships.

Ageism hides behind language too.

In the "Okay, Boomer" phenomenon, we see ageism at work via social media.

"Okay, Boomer" is a reactionary societal defensive mechanism born from frustration. The question is, why wouldn't younger people become frustrated at leaders, bosses, parents, politicians, and professionals who (for most of their young working life) have condescended to them?

Older generations mock Millennials as a participation trophy generation and label Gen Z as children. Legitimate conversation cannot happen when we distill people down to their generational age and stereotypes. Both emerging generations and established generations contribute to the issues. Finding solutions will take honest, healthy, and bold leaders from both sides to heal the divide.

A generational gap is a natural phenomenon, but ageism is a societal ill. This book is an attempt to train leaders to lead one another through the emotional, mental, and economic minefield that is the generational gap —especially when and where ageism (in any direction) exists.

Great leaders create community through shared culture and core values.

We must clarify our values, and it is not a one-time declaration.

We must continually create shared culture through acculturation, not assimilation.

That takes awareness, intention, and action.

This takes higher leadership.

CHAPTER 10: A CALL TO HIGHER LEADERSHIP

"A leader is best when people barely know he exists, when his work is done, his aim fulfilled, they will say: we did it ourselves."

- Lao Tzu, legendary founder of Taoism and author of *The Tao Te Ching*

SERVANT LEADERSHIP

"The great leader is seen as servant first."

-Robert K. Greenleaf

The above quote challenges traditional leadership models. Servant leadership is a leadership philosophy in which the primary goal of the leader is to serve. It differs from traditional leadership, where the leader's focus is on the success of their company or organizations. The servant-leader is always a servant first. This form of leadership begins with the natural feeling that one wants to serve. It focuses on offering service to others. Servant leadership is not an entirely new concept or a way to lead, but it hasn't become popular vernacular until recent decades. Some consider this to be the highest form of leadership.

At Paradigm Shift, we take it a step further.

"Leadership without servanthood is simply manipulation." - Paradigm Shift

Leadership *is* serving others. It is about making situations better for everyone involved. Not just the stockholders, the owners, or the C-suite.

Consider this.

If you are leading others in a way that doesn't serve (or help) those who you are leading, what are you doing? You are, in some way, self-serving, which is a subtle form of manipulation.

You are using your followers.

You are manipulating your followers for something other than their best interest.

We see this all the time in the world around us.

We can do better.

John Maxwell wrote that servant leadership is the highest calling.[50] I believe it is the purpose of every leader to pour into people so they can become better versions of themselves, and they, in turn, can do the same for others.

We may make money for our company.

---

[50] https://www.johnmaxwell.com/blog/live2lead-a-chance-to-serve-your-people-and-your-community/

We may strategically add to our board's portfolio.

But do others willingly follow us?

All the conversation in the book is unnecessary.

You and I don't *have* to be good leaders, better leaders, cross-generational leaders.

But we can be.

We have the opportunity to be.

The ideas in this book aren't easy and they come with a price tag.

Higher leadership has a higher cost.

It also has higher rewards.

LOYALTY RETENTION

This call to higher leadership requires us to look beyond generational stereotypes and discover an individual's worldview.

Higher leadership is seeking first to understand. We seek to understand why people do what they do.

Good leadership is seeking the why, understanding the why, and shaping the why.

Great leadership is becoming the why.

When we answer the call to higher leadership, we become the why behind people's reasons.

We are the reason someone loves their job.

We are the reason they give their best.

We are the reason that conflict is resolved, people feel valued, and the company thrives.

Great leaders create a following of people willing to go the extra mile, because they go the extra mile.

Great leaders think of how their decisions affect more than the bottom line.

Great leaders consider the individuals' needs and the group's goals.

When we serve those we lead, they become loyal to more than our company; they become loyal to us.

They begin to take emotional, mental, and creative ownership of their role and in the work they produce.

As you encourage ideas, they bring new ideas to the table.

As you empower them to make decisions, they become decision makers.

As you encourage ingenuity, they become the geneses of action.

A servant leader takes ownership of their faults and works with humility toward improvement: in themselves first and their squad next. A servant leader does not require from others anything she would not demand from herself.

Leadership without servanthood is *simply* manipulation.

Our people should forever be the focus of any business venture.

They are our market, our workforce, and our most excellent resource.

This book is not a how-to-deal-with-old-fogeys or how-can-we-whip-young-people-into-shape kind of book.

This book is not a quick way to solve generational conflicts.

It is a call to higher leadership.

As a culture, we tend to lump all of a generation into a stereotypical mold and then complain about the shape of the world — the one we molded.

If we truly want change in the world, we must stop this lazy practice.

What if we all — emerging generations and established generations — committed to combine our worldview and work together toward a common goal?

What would the world look like then?

We certainly need change.

Change is complaining.

Change is more than shouting or protesting.

Change takes work.

It will take thousands of hours of work, collaboration, and conversation within the established constructs — social, governmental, and economical — to create a better future.

On the micro-scale, change can be in your office, and on the macro-scale, it can be worldwide.

The key is you.

YOU ARE A LEADER.

We have always had a generational gap.

There will always be a gap…ask Socrates or John Adams.

There won't always be you.

You are the solution.

You are the leader we need.

Now, go get 'em, kid.

ABOUT THE AUTHOR

Jerrod Murr is a speaker, leadership facilitator, and cultural entrepreneur. Murr is the co-founder of Paradigm Shift, a leadership development company focused on bringing out the best in people. The Paradigm Shift team delivers keynotes, workshops, and retreats to groups of all levels. We partner with teams to improve interpersonal communication, team dynamics, and individual leadership. *(Okay, if you have read this far, you are really interested and we appreciate it. If you like the book and any ideas shared, please reach out at www.PS.company. We would love to work with you or your team, school, church, or company. We love what we do. We love to share it with folks like you.)* Back to Jerrod. He is a small-town kid from Muskogee, OK. He still lives there on a ranch with his wife, Jenn, two daughters Adelae and Josalyn, and son, Everett. They even host executive retreats on the ranch. You should check those out. Murr's favorite book is The Giving Tree, he won a game show, and was once detained in Cuba.

Need a speaker? Want to bring this material to your team?

Stay up to date with all things Jerrod and 8-track to Emoji by visiting his website.

www.jerrodmurr.co

www.ps.company

I'd love to connect. Let's be friends! Scan the QR code to be directed to my Instagram.

@jerrodmurr

Jerrod Murr

Jerrod Anthony Murr

VOCΛ Jerrod Murr

Printed in the USA
CPSIA information can be obtained
at www.ICGtesting.com
CBHW051514061024
15164CB00002B/7